Expectations, Employment and Prices

ROGER E. A. FARMER

Expectations, Employment and Prices

OXFORD
UNIVERSITY PRESS
2010

OXFORD
UNIVERSITY PRESS

Oxford University Press, Inc., publishes works that further
Oxford University's objective of excellence
in research, scholarship, and education.

Oxford   New York
Auckland   Cape Town   Dar es Salaam   Hong Kong   Karachi
Kuala Lumpur   Madrid   Melbourne   Mexico City   Nairobi
New Delhi   Shanghai   Taipei   Toronto

With offices in
Argentina   Austria   Brazil   Chile   Czech Republic   France   Greece
Guatemala   Hungary   Italy   Japan   Poland   Portugal   Singapore
South Korea   Switzerland   Thailand   Turkey   Ukraine   Vietnam

Published by Oxford University Press, Inc.
198 Madison Avenue, New York, NY 10016

www.oup.com

Oxford is a registered trademark of Oxford University Press.

Library of Congress Cataloging-in-Publication Data
Farmer, Roger E. A.
Expectations, employment and prices / Roger E. A. Farmer.
    p. cm.
Includes bibliographical references and index.
ISBN 978-0-19-539790-1
1. Unemployment-Econometric models. 2. Unemployment-Effect
of monetary policy on. 3. Capital market. 4. Equilibrium
(Economics) 5. Rational expectations (Economic theory)
I. Title.
HD5707.5.F37   2010
331.13'7—dc22   2009024295

9 8 7 6 5 4 3 2 1

Printed in the United States of America
on acid-free paper

To Roxanne, my inspiration.

PREFACE

I HAVE LONG BELIEVED that modern interpreters of Keynes missed the main point of The General Theory; high unemployment is an equilibrium phenomenon that can persist for a very long time if nothing is done by a government to correct the problem. This was the point of my 1984 paper, which argued that the natural rate hypothesis is false. In the intervening years, I have had time to refine this idea. This book is the culmination of my thought process.

I began thinking about a book on Keynesian economics, based on a search theory of the labor market, in 2003. I have had many conversations with friends and colleagues along the way and the question I hear again and again is, Why write a book? It has become the norm for serious economists to convey their ideas in articles. There is a benefit to this approach since publishing an idea in a journal subjects it to a process of peer review. But there is also a downside to publishing in refereed journals, particularly when the goal is as ambitious as the project that I am engaged in. Even the very best journals (perhaps particularly the very best journals) are biased toward publishing very good articles that contribute to what Thomas Kuhn, in his 1962 book *The Structure of Scientific Revolutions*, called "normal science." A successful article in a top journal takes an established paradigm and solves a puzzle that researchers can identify as a valid question. I have a more ambitious goal: I want to overturn a way of thinking that has been established among macroeconomists for twenty years. The rejection of several different core assumptions at the same time poses a problem if one wants to publish journal articles since the pieces stand or fall together and there is no space in a twenty-page article to explain why.

I have always found in writing research papers that no idea is ever complete, and the same is true of a book, but more so. As this project developed, I added new pieces and changed old ones. The project gained new urgency when the world economy began to disintegrate at an alarming rate in the fall of 2008. I decided at that point that it was important to publish the ideas in whatever form they were currently in and to worry about polishing them later. The theory I develop here has direct relevance to the world economic crisis and it suggests a new and potentially important solution to the problem of maintaining global stability.

Expectations, Employment and Prices is aimed at economists in academia and policy institutions, and the general reader will find it abstract. It is full of equations, theorems, definitions, and proofs that may be intimidating to the nonspecialist. For better or worse, that is the way the language of academic articles has developed. The benefit of abstraction is that by phrasing arguments in this way, one is able to lay bare the logic that underlies one's conclusions. But the ideas are not so difficult as to be beyond the grasp of the average reader. For that reason, I have written a second book on the same topic that translates my arguments into English. This second book, *How the Economy Works: Confidence, Crashes and Self-Fulfilling Prophecies*, will appear shortly after *Expectations*, and I hope it will influence the policy debate on the development of new institutions to prevent economic crises of the kind we are witnessing as I write this Preface in December 2008.

Many people have helped me to develop my ideas. I am grateful to my brother-in-law Ray Barrell and my late sister Mary K. Farmer for nurturing my early love of and interest in economics. I have benefited tremendously from interactions with colleagues and students: Andy Atkeson, Arnold Harberger, Amy Brown, Ariel Burstein, Anton Cheremukhin, Hal Cole, Matthias Doepke, Corey Garriott, Gary Hansen, Christian Hellwig, Andrew Hollenhorst, Masanori Kashiwagi, Axel Leijhonhufrud, Hanno Lustig, Lee Ohanian, Paulina Restrepo, Karl Shell, Pierre-Olivier Weill, and Mark Wright have all, directly or indirectly, influenced the final product. I have worked with many coauthors over the past twenty-five years. Jess Benhabib, Rosalind Bennett, Andreas Beyer, Jang Ting Guo, Jerome Henry, Amartya Lahiri, Massimiliano Marcellino, Kazuo Nishimura, Daniel Waggoner, Ralph Winter, Michael Woodford, and Tao Zha have all influenced my thinking in one way or another and indirectly contributed to the ideas in this book. Thank you all. Alain Venditti and

Carine Nourry of the University of Aix-Marseilles worked with me on a stochastic model that influenced Chapter 9. I am grateful for their hospitality during a visit to Marseilles in the summer of 2008. Riccardo DiCecio from the St. Louis Fed, Marco Guerrazzi of the University of Pisa, and Colin Rogers of the University of Adelaide gave me comments and corrections on an earlier draft, and Masanori Kashiwagi has read and criticized the entire manuscript. I thank all of them for helping me to weed out mistakes, although I am sure that some remain. I thank Martin Wolf of the Finacial Times for providing me with an important platform over the past several months that enabled me to reach a larger audience to seriously consider my ideas. Thanks to Dave Cass and Karl Shell, who introduced me to sunspots, an idea that they published in 1983 in the *Journal of Political Economy*, and to Costas Azariadis, who introduced me to the idea of a self-fulfilling prophecy both through personal discussions and in his 1981 *Journal of Economic Theory* article. The early 1980s was a wonderful time to be at the University of Pennsylvania. I am grateful to the National Science Foundation, which has supported my research for many years with a series of grants that gave me the freedom to think independently and to develop new ideas. Most recently, I was awarded grant #SBR 0720839, which helped to support the research developed in this book.

I thank Terry Vaughn and the entire team at Oxford University Press for their dedication and assistance throughout this project. My greatest debt is to my wife, Roxanne, and my son, Leland, for their loving support and encouragement for many years.

CONTENTS

PART I

THE THEORY OF
UNEMPLOYMENT

THE FIRST FOUR CHAPTERS of this book develop a theory of the
macroeconomy that brings the central ideas of Keynesian economics
up to date with modern macroeconomics. Chapter 1 presents an outline
of the book. Chapters 2, 3, and 4 develop a model of the economy that
explains why unregulated capitalist economies may deliver inefficient
outcomes. Chapter 2 presents a basic model of the labor market, Chapter
3 extends this model to multiple goods, and Chapter 4 adds saving and
investment.

CHAPTER 1 | **What This Book Is About**

Those who cannot remember the past are condemned to repeat it.

—George Santayana, *The Life of Reason* (1905)

T HIS BOOK IS ABOUT the business cycle and how to control it. I will explain why major recessions occur and how government policy can and should be used to maintain high and stable employment. The reasoning I will provide is inspired by Keynesian economics and is based on ideas from *The General Theory of Employment, Interest and Money* (1936). Importantly however, I go beyond the ideas in Keynes' book by providing a microfoundation to the concept that the equilibrium level of unemployment may be inefficient. I will argue that government can and should intervene in markets to maintain a high and stable level of employment. Some of the remedies I will propose are standard and part of the current arsenal of policies employed by the governments of all market economies. Some remedies are new and involve extensions of the institutions that were developed in the wake of the publication of *The General Theory*.

What is new in my assessment of standard remedies is a theory of individual behavior that explains why fiscal and monetary policies are appropriate and how they work. A byproduct of my extension of Keynesian models is an explanation of how inflation and unemployment can occur together and a theory of what it means to maintain full employment. My extension of Keynesian theory gives rise to a policy suggestion that involves an expansion of the role of the asset market management that has been conducted more or less actively since the inception of the Federal Reserve system in 1913. I will argue that the Fed should intervene to prevent both asset market bubbles and stock market crashes. Rather than simply raising or lowering the treasury bill rate through purchases and sales of T-bills, this would require active participation in the stock market through the support of the price of an index fund. I explain this idea in Chapter 11.

Although economic fluctuations in the U.S. have been relatively mild in recent decades, during the Great Depression of the 1930s the unemployment rate exceeded 20% for a protracted period of time. The Great Depression is not unique, and similar episodes have been a recurrent feature of capitalist economies since the beginning of the industrial revolution. Timothy Kehoe and Edward Prescott (2007) define a great depression to be a period of diminished economic output with at least one year where output is 20% below the trend. According to this definition, Argentina, Brazil, Chile, and Mexico have all experienced great depressions since 1980.

What causes big fluctuations in economic activity? For several decades following the publication of *The General Theory*, economists thought they had an answer; the Great Depression was a failure of an unregulated capitalist economy to efficiently utilize available resources. But with the resurgence of classical ideas in the 1970s, the key premise of *The General Theory*, that market economies are not inherently self-stabilizing, has been called into question. Although there has been a recent resurgence of Keynesian ideas under the rubric of "new-Keynesian economics," the models studied by the new-Keynesians are hybrids that incorporate a classical core. New-Keynesian models allow for temporary deviations of unemployment from its "natural rate" as a consequence of sticky prices, but they contain a stabilizing mechanism that causes a return to the natural rate over time. Since the return to the steady state is typically rapid in these models, the welfare costs of business cycles are also small and arise from second-order consequences of deviating from the social planning optimum.[1]

This book is different. All of the models I will describe reject the natural rate hypothesis and treat the unemployment rate as a variable that is determined in equilibrium by aggregate demand.

In his 1966 book, Axel Leijonhufvud made the distinction between Keynesian economics and the economics of Keynes. The neoclassical synthesis is the interpretation of *The General Theory* that was introduced by Samuelson (1955) in the third edition of his undergraduate textbook. According to this view, the economy is Keynesian in the short run, when prices have not yet adjusted. It is classical in the long run, after price adjustments have run their course. Leijonhufvud pointed out that the assumption that *The General Theory* is about sticky prices is central to this orthodox interpretation of Keynesian economics, but it is not a central argument of the text of *The General Theory*.

This book provides an alternative microfoundation to Keynesian economics that does not rely on sticky prices. In successive chapters, I construct a series of models that build on a single idea. Each of them is constructed around a conventional general equilibrium model in which real resources must be used to move unemployed workers into jobs using a "search technology." Although this technology is convex, I assume that the planning optimum cannot be decentralized as a competitive equilibrium because moral hazard prevents the creation of markets for the search inputs. As an alternative, I introduce an equilibrium concept called demand-constrained equilibrium, in which the level of economic activity is determined by self-fulfilling crises of confidence. I refer to the resulting model as "old-Keynesian" to differentiate it from new-Keynesian economics that incorporates the natural rate hypothesis of Milton Friedman (1968) and Edmund Phelps (1968). In contrast to new-Keynesian models, those described in this book display multiple stationary perfect foresight equilibria, and there is a different stationary unemployment rate for each possible level of beliefs.

1.1 The Nature of the Enquiry

The fact that great depressions occur relatively frequently in Western economies suggests that unregulated capitalist economies sometimes go very wrong: This viewpoint is, however, controversial. Some observers have suggested that the Great Depression of the 1930s in the US was an aberration. Economists who take this view point to postwar U.S. experience in which unemployment has been relatively low and business cycles relatively mild for long periods of time. But Kehoe and Prescott (2007) cite at least four episodes of great depressions in western economies in the past twenty-five years. These episodes require an explanation that is consistent with our understanding of the functioning of the macroeconomy in more normal times.

According to Keynes, the Great Depression was evidence of the systemic failure of unregulated markets to deliver an efficient level of employment. According to this view, government can and should intervene to maintain a high level of employment. An alternative view that has recently been regaining popularity is that great depressions are caused by the interference of government regulatory bodies in the smooth functioning of markets. An early example of this view is the book by Milton Friedman and Anna Schwartz (1963), which argued that the Great Depression in the U.S. was caused by incompetent monetary policy in the 1920s. More recently, Cole and Ohanian (2004) have argued that Herbert Hoover's regulatory policies deepened the depression in the early 1930s. This is a remarkable turn of intellectual thought from the prevailing mood in the early postwar period, when President Richard Nixon was famously quoted as saying, "We are all Keynesians now."[2]

A prevalent view of business cycles in the economics profession is that of real business cycles according to which most economic fluctuations are caused by unforeseen shocks to total factor productivity. According to this view, the market system is efficient and the allocation of resources in a laissez faire economy is, to a first approximation, a reflection of the allocation that would be made by a benevolent social planner whose goal is to maximize social welfare. This view is more extreme than that which Keynes ascribed to the "classical economists" of whom he considered Pigou a prime example. Pigou (1929), Lavington (1922), and Haberler (1937) all recognized a role for total factor productivity, but they also recognized alternative sources of aggregate fluctuation including "errors of optimism and pessimism," "harvest variations," and "autonomous monetary movements" (1929, Chapter 22). In *Industrial Fluctuations*, Pigou concludes that although "... the popular opinion that industrial fluctuations as such *must* be social evils is invalid," nevertheless, "... industrial fluctuations produced in the ways described [above] are certainly social evils."

The General Theory makes a break from 1920s business cycle theory by separating the theory of distribution from the theory of aggregate economic activity. Although Keynes believed that the market system was probably an efficient way of deciding which kinds of goods were produced for a given volume of employment, he argued that unregulated capitalist systems did not produce an efficient allocation of labor. His arguments had an important influence on political economy and resulted in the current state-capitalist system in which the monetary and fiscal authorities in most Western democracies are charged with the objective of maintaining a high and stable level of employment. The fiscal and monetary policy environment since 1940 has been very different from that of the 1920s and 1930s *as a direct consequence* of ideas that arose from the publication of *The General Theory*, and hence it is invalid to use the postwar period as an example of the success of the market system. Rather, it represents prima facie evidence for the success of Keynesian economics.

A good example is provided by the U.S. economy. In 1929 federal and state taxes together accounted for 11% of GDP, but by 1999 that figure had risen to 36%. When the Fed was created in 1913, policymakers had little conception of how to run a successful monetary policy, and for most of the 1930s the short-term interest rate was too low to be used as an effective instrument of control. Since 1945, however, the size of government has been large enough to create an automatic stabilizing mechanism that generates budget deficits in recessions and budget surpluses in expansions. Further, the Fed actively pursues a countercyclical monetary policy by lowering the interest rate during recessions and raising it during expansions. These are exactly the policies that Keynes argued for in the 1930s, and it is ironic that the success of these very policies should be seen by some as evidence against the theories that spawned them.

1.2 The Theory Summarized

Although the current volume is heavily influenced by *The General Theory*, it is not a simple translation of that book into the language of modern economics. Seventy years of history since the publication of *The General Theory* have produced data that invalidate at least some of its key themes. Most notable among these is the experience of stagflation in the 1970s that is inconsistent with the "reverse L" theory of aggregate supply outlined in Chapter 21 of *The General Theory*, which explained Keynes's theory of prices.

There are two key ideas in *The General Theory* that set it apart from pre-Keynesian economics: The first is that there is something distinctive about the labor market that makes the marginal disutility of labor different in general from the real wage. The second is that aggregate economic activity is determined by the "animal spirits" of investors. This book will preserve both of these ideas, modified in a way that respects recent developments in dynamic general equilibrium theory. The integration of dynamics into modern economic theory provides a set of mathematical tools that enable me to bring dynamic ideas into Keynesian macroeconomics in a way that was not possible in the 1930s.

The ideas that I have identified as central to Keynesian economics can be separated into theories of aggregate supply and aggregate demand. Although the form with which I will state these ideas is different from existing interpretations of *The General Theory*, the intellectual predecessors are those formulated by Keynes in 1936, who expressed the following sentiment in a 1937 article in response to his critics:

> I am more attached to the comparatively simple fundamental ideas that underlie my theory than to the particular forms in which I have embodied them, and have no desire that the latter should be crystallized at the present stage of the debate. If the simplest basic ideas can become familiar and acceptable, time and experience and the collaboration of a number of minds will discover the best way of expressing them. (Keynes, 1937, pp. 211–212)

The following two sections outline briefly my main arguments and explain how they are related to the "fundamental ideas" of *The General Theory*.

1.3 The Theory of Aggregate Supply

Chapter 2 presents a reformulation of the theory of aggregate supply. Keynes's theory has been widely criticized for its lack of microfoundations, and it is often asserted that if the marginal disutility of labor is not equal to the real wage, as Keynes assumed in Chapter 2 of *The General Theory*, then unemployed workers would be expected to offer to work for a lower wage. This argument is based on the implicit assumption that the labor market is an auction in which unemployed workers can effectively signal their willingness to work for profit-maximizing firms.

Following arguments by Patinkin (1956) and Clower (1965), the disequilibrium literature of the, '70s, exemplified by Barro and Grossman (1971), Benassy (1975), and Malinvaud (1977), tried to address this

point by constructing an explicit theory of transactions at disequilibrium prices. This literature was ultimately judged to be unsuccessful
by a generation of economists who followed the equilibrium approach
of Lucas and Rapping (1969) and Lucas (1972). Although there were
contemporary writers (Axel Leijonhufvud [1966] is a leading example)
who claimed that Keynesian economics was never about "sticky prices,"
Leijonhufvud and his contemporaries never managed to formulate an
alternative theory that was capable of answering the new-Classical criticism that disequilibrium theory is empty. This argument rested on the fact
that it contains what Lucas called "free parameters" and comes down to
the claim that, as a consequence, the theory is untestable.

In this book, I pick up on the recent literature developed by Shimer
(2005) and Hall (2005) that follows earlier work in search theory.
Pissarides (2000) provides an excellent summary. In this literature, it
is assumed that the process by which an unemployed worker finds a
job requires the input of resources on the part of the firm and time on
the part of the worker. When a worker and a firm meet, they determine
the wage to be paid through a Nash bargain. Shimer pointed out that
this assumption does not provide a good quantitative explanation of
employment fluctuations, and Hall proposed to replace it with an alternative wage determination mechanism. He assumed that the real wage
is determined one period in advance. Shimer's criticism has generated
a considerable amount of recent work by researchers who are exploring
alternative wage determination mechanisms in an attempt to reconcile
the volatility of vacancies and unemployment with a model in which
economic fluctuations are driven by productivity shocks.

Since the work of Diamond (1982, 1984), it has been known that
there are often multiple equilibria in labor search models, and since
the work of Howitt (1986) and Howitt and McAfee (1987), it has been
known that there may be a continuum of equilibria. The response of most
economists has been to try to resolve this indeterminacy by adding a new
fundamental equation. The use of the Nash bargaining equation, with a
fixed bargaining weight, is an example of one such addition.

In this book, I take an alternative approach. I develop a series of
models in which the labor market is cleared by search, but instead of
closing it with an explicit bargaining assumption, I assume only that all
firms must offer the same wage. This leads to a new theory in which
there are many wages, all of which are consistent with a zero profit
equilibrium, and it provides a microfounded analog of Keynes's idea that
there are many levels of economic activity at which the macroeconomy

may be in equilibrium. To select an equilibrium and close the model, I introduce the idea that households form beliefs about the future value of productive capital and I show that for any sequence of self-fulfilling beliefs, less than a given bound, there exists a Keynesian equilibrium. This equilibrium will in general be inefficient in the sense that a benevolent social planner would prefer a different employment level that may be higher or lower. Hence, I am able to articulate the Keynesian story of the Great Depression in a model with well-defined microfoundations in which no individual agent has an incentive to deviate from his or her chosen action.

1.4 The Theory of Aggregate Demand

In addition to his theory of aggregate supply, Keynes contributed a theory of effective demand based on the multiplier. Problems with this theory were already apparent in the 1950s, when it was realized that estimates of the marginal propensity to consume were typically much lower in cross-section than time series data. This led to Friedman's (1957) book, *A Theory of the Consumption Function*, in which he proposed the concept of permanent income as a way of resolving the disparity between different estimates. But this was not the only important debate that characterized the macroeconomics of the immediate postwar period.

The exercise of providing a dynamic foundation to Keynesian economics led to an attack on the intellectual foundations of the multiplier and a debate over the effectiveness of fiscal policy. Some economists have argued, on purely theoretical grounds, that one dollar of expenditure by government might, under some circumstances, perfectly "crowd out" one dollar of private consumption expenditure and aggregate demand would be unaltered. The debate was ultimately resolved by recognizing that crowding out would occur only if government bonds were not perceived as net wealth by the community as a whole, although this debate, and other preoccupations of the postwar Keynesian economists, became irrelevant when Keynesian economics was replaced by the real business cycle paradigm.[3]

In this book, I will breathe new life into many of the old debates. I will construct a microfoundation to the theory of aggregate demand based on the assumption that agents are forward looking with rational expectations of future prices. Although this is a departure from Keynes's theory of expectations, it is a departure worth making since it allows me to directly compare the implications of the theory with modern neoclassical alternatives.

Keynes believed that some forms of uncertainty cannot be quantified and that agents must act on the basis of partial information. Although the agents in my model will be able to form probability distributions over future events, not all of these events will be fundamental in the sense in which that word is now used in general equilibrium theory to describe uncertainty due to changes in preferences, endowments, and technology. Although these sources of uncertainty may be present in the models I describe in this book, in addition, agents will be required to form expectations of the future actions of others. It is here that I capture the Keynesian idea of the importance of "animal spirits".

If investors today believe that all future investors will be pessimistic, then this belief will be self-fulfilling. In contrast to the previous formulations of this idea that I described in my work with Jess Benhabib (1994) and Jang Ting Guo (1994, 1995) and summarized in my book *The Macroeconomics of Self-Fulfilling Prophecies* (1999), agents in the models I will describe in the following chapters may form self-fulfilling beliefs that lead to an increase in the unemployment rate in the steady state.

1.5 A Road Map to the Book

This book is divided into three parts. Part I presents the basic theory of the labor market and it consists of this introduction plus three more chapters. Chapter 2 presents the simplest version of my main idea— a microfounded model of a labor market, based on search theory, in which there exists a continuum of steady-state equilibria. This chapter is essential reading. Chapter 3 develops a model with multiple goods. It provides what I believe to be an interesting insight into the methods used here and originally developed by Keynes. Unlike all of modern macroeconomics, Keynesian economics has no need of the concept of a production function. This notion, which is central to a theory based on classical reasoning, is not missing because it was forgotten; it is missing because it is not needed. Keynesian economics determines employment and the money value of GDP. Although it is possible to extend the theory to explain the physical units of commodities that are produced in any period, this extension is not needed to understand the concept of an equilibrium at less than full employment.

Chapter 4 was written early in the development of this book. It was an attempt to use the search framework that I developed in chapters 2 and 3 to provide a microfounded account of the Keynesian idea of the multiplier. Keynes thought that investors and savers have different motives, and he argued that investment is the driving force behind business fluctuations. This chapter reflects that idea. It is possible to make sense of the multiplier within the framework of this book, but as the project developed I realized that a dynamic theory of aggregate demand can provide a different interpretation of the Keynesian story of the Great Depression in which consumption depends on wealth rather than income. The Keynesian multiplier is a fundamentally static concept and the idea of separating investors and savers does not work well within an intertemporal equilibrium model. I nevertheless decided to leave this chapter as part of the final manuscript since it makes clear that fiscal intervention relies on a distribution effect between different generations. This theme will be important later in the book when I discuss the effectiveness of fiscal policy in two alternative models with long-lived agents.

The second part of the book breaks new ground. In Chapter 5, I argue that most modern macroeconomists have defined away what is arguably the most interesting macroeconomic question: Why does unemployment move closely with the components of aggregate demand at medium to low frequencies? I became interested in this question after my collaboration with Andreas Beyer (2007) in which we studied the time series properties of the unemployment rate. It is a question that has been ignored for two reasons. First, real business cycle (RBC) economists do not try to explain the unemployment rate at all; instead, their models contain total hours worked as án index of labor market activity. Although I see this as a deficiency of RBC theory, it is not a serious one since hours worked move closely with unemployment. More important, much of recent data analysis by macroeconomists accepts an argument by Robert Hodrick and Edward C. Prescott (1997), who claimed that the interesting facts to explain are deviations of time series on employment, investment consumption, and GDP from a flexible trend. This use of their detrending method leads economists who follow this approach to miss correlations between employment and consumption at medium frequencies.[4] These movements are important to study since, if my theory is correct, they have large consequences for welfare. Chapter 5 explains an alternative detrending procedure that reveals a new and arguably more interesting set of facts to be explained by the theory. This chapter is essential to understanding my claims for the empirical relevance of my ideas.

Chapters 6, 7, and 8 apply the detrending methods of Chapter 5 to view the data defined in this way through the lens of theory. Chapter 6 builds a rudimentary infinite horizon model to explain the facts of the Great Depression. Chapter 7 elaborates on it by adding a richer population structure to explain the wartime recovery, and Chapter 8 studies data from 1951 through 2000. Each of these chapters stands alone as a description of a particular episode from economic history and together they develop a narrative account that views the facts in a new way. Although the explanations I give of the depression and the recovery will be familiar, my interpretation of the postwar data is new. I interpret the slow-growth decade of the 1970s as a demand-induced slowdown as opposed to the usual supply-side explanation.

In Part III, I turn from the theory of unemployment to the theory of prices. Chapter 9 adds money to a stochastic monetary version of the representative agent model from Chapter 6. Chapter 10 uses this model to explain how inflation and unemployment can occur together and it argues that this fact should not lead us to give up on important ideas that form the basis of *The General Theory*: notably, that unregulated capitalist economies can be inefficient in the steady state and that noneconomic fundamentals can influence economic activity. In Chapter 11, I argue for the design of a new monetary policy for the 21st century. The Fed should conduct open market operations in a portfolio of assets by buying and selling shares in an index fund of stock market securities. Its goal would be to peg the value of this fund to prevent excessive market movements either up or down.

CHAPTER 2 | The Basic Model

THIS CHAPTER DEVELOPS a one-sector model that explains the theme of the book: that inefficiently high levels of unemployment can exist in steady-state equilibrium. The chapter builds on earlier work (2008b) published in a volume in honor of Axel Leijonhufvud. I develop a model, based on a labor market theory in which the search inputs of workers and firms are combined to produce matches. A match is an employed worker in place at a firm. Search requires two inputs: (1) the time spent searching by workers and (2) the resources needed to post vacancies by firms. Most existing search models do not assume that these inputs are traded in competitive markets. Instead, they assume that vacancies and unemployed workers are matched randomly. If searching workers and vacancy posting firms take the real wage as given, the resulting general equilibrium model has fewer equations than unknowns.

In search models, it is typical to assume that the match technology satisfies standard neoclassical properties of monotonicity, differentiability, and constant returns to scale. These assumptions allow one to prove versions of the first and second welfare theorems in a general equilibrium model with search: every competitive equilibrium is Pareto optimal, and every Pareto optimal allocation can be decentralized as a competitive equilibrium. But what might this decentralization look like?

The natural decentralization would posit the existence of a large number of competitive employment agencies. Each agency would operate a match technology and would purchase search inputs from firms and workers. The agency would purchase, from an unemployed worker, the exclusive right to match that worker with a vacancy. From a firm with a vacant job, the agency would purchase the right to match that vacancy with an unemployed worker. The agency would operate a matching process and resell the joint product, a worker–firm match, back to the worker–firm pair.

Why is this decentralization implausible? First, it involves transactions that we do not observe in the real world. There are no private institutions that pay money to unemployed workers for the right to find them jobs. Nor do we find the widespread use of private employment agencies that pay firms for the privilege of acting as their recruiting agents. A moment's reflection suggests that these markets do not exist because of the moral hazard associated with monitoring the motives of the participants. Efficient operation of these markets requires exclusivity of contracts. If such markets existed, it would be difficult or impossible to prevent an unemployed worker from selling the exclusive right to be matched to multiple agencies and to turn down job offers when presented on spurious but hard-to-monitor grounds. Since there may be legitimate reasons to refuse a job, the requirement that all potential matches must be accepted is not a feasible solution to this problem. Casual observation of state-run employment agencies suggests that this problem is present in practice and is a significant impediment to the efficient operation of a matching market.

2.1 Components of the Theory

The model of this chapter is inspired by Keynes's *General Theory*. In that book, Keynes claimed that the real wage is not equated to the marginal disutility of labor and he introduced the principle of effective demand. These ideas are important and they have guided several generations of policy. This chapter is an attempt to make sense of them in a micro-founded theory of labor market search.

2.1.1 RELATIONSHIP TO KEYNES

In *The General Theory*, effective demand is driven primarily by the "animal spirits" of investors. Animal spirits are a key component of autonomous investment expenditure, which in turn, is the prime cause of fluctuations in effective demand. To capture this idea, one requires a dynamic model since investment involves plans that span at least two periods. However, autonomous expenditure is also determined by government spending, and by recognizing this, I will be able to explain how a search model of the labor market can be embedded into general equilibrium in a relatively simple environment: a one-period model that abstracts from capital in which output and employment are driven by fiscal policy.

The one-period model I will describe is simpler than the first dynamic model that I introduce in Chapter 4 since I abstract from capital and assume that all output is produced from labor. Sections 2.1.2 and 2.1.3 are about the microeconomic behaviors of households and firms. The questions I study are not ones that occupied Keynes, who was concerned solely with relationships between aggregates. But they are questions that I will need to address in an enquiry that seeks to provide microfoundations to Keynes's concepts of aggregate demand and supply. Initially, I will simplify the environment by studying a model in which there is a single period, a single commodity, and a large number of identical households and firms. These are not simplifications found in *The General Theory* and, as I will show in Chapter 3, they are unnecessary simplifications if one is interested in a comparative static view of macroeconomic activity.

Keynes took the existing stocks of capital and existing nominal wages as historically determined and showed how effective demand would determine economic activity. My goals are more comprehensive. I want, to demonstrate how the principle of effective demand can be consistent with individual behavior at a point in time. Beyond that, I want to link the periods in a dynamic general equilibrium model where the people in my model form rational expectations of future events. Although the single-agent, single-good fiction is unnecessary to explain effective demand in a comparative static model, it considerably simplifies the nature of aggregate dynamics.

2.1.2 HOUSEHOLDS

The model consists of a unit mass of families, each of which has a unit mass of members. These assumptions allow me to abstract from the fact that unemployed workers are typically worse off than employed workers. In this model, the family self-insures its unfortunate members. The utility of the family is represented by an increasing concave function j,

$$J = j(C), \tag{2.1}$$

where J represents the utility of the family's consumption, C. Since all families are identical, I will refer to the consumption of an individual family and to aggregate consumption with the same symbol.

Each family has a measure 1 of workers, all of whom begin the period unemployed. Leisure has no utility and each household solves the problem

$$\max_{\{C,H\}} j\,(C) \tag{2.2}$$

such that

$$pC \leq wL\,(1-\tau) + TR, \tag{2.3}$$

$$H \leq 1, \tag{2.4}$$

$$L = \tilde{q}H, \tag{2.5}$$

$$U = H - L. \tag{2.6}$$

Equation (2.3) is a budget constraint. Each family's consumption is constrained by its after-tax employment income. w is the money wage, p is the money price, L is the measure of employed workers, τ is the tax rate, and TR is a lump-sum transfer, measured in dollars. H represents the measure of household members that search for employment, and Equation (2.4) constrains this to be no greater than 1, the household size. The measure of household members that successfully find jobs is represented by $\tilde{q}H$, where $\tilde{q}$ is taken as given by the household in a search market equilibrium; Equation (2.5) is the relationship between employment and search. Finally, Equation (2.6) defines the measure of unemployed, U, to be those searching workers who do not find jobs. This problem has the trivial solution

$$H = 1, \tag{2.7}$$

$$pC = wL\,(1-\tau) + TR, \tag{2.8}$$

$$L = \tilde{q}. \tag{2.9}$$

Since there is no utility to leisure, all workers look for a job, and since there is no motive to save, all income is consumed.

2.1.3 FIRMS

Firms produce output using a constant returns-to-scale technology in which labor is the sole input. There is free entry and each firm solves the problem

$$\max_{\{V,Y,L,X\}} pY - wL \tag{2.10}$$

such that

$$Y \leq AX, \tag{2.11}$$

$$X + V = L, \tag{2.12}$$

$$L = qV. \tag{2.13}$$

Equation (2.11) is the production function: Y is output, $A > 0$ is a productivity parameter, and X is the measure of workers employed by the firm in direct production. A firm that employs L workers may allocate them to produce commodities (this is the measure X) or to the recruiting department (this is the measure V). A firm that devotes V workers to recruiting will hire qV workers, where q is taken as given by the firm.

I have assumed that labor, rather than output, is used to post vacancies, in contrast to most search models. This innovation is not important and is made for expositional simplicity and to allow me, later in the book, to write down models that can easily be compared with more familiar real business cycle economies. The timing of the employment decision deserves some discussion since it allows the firm to use workers to recruit themselves.

If a firm begins the period with no workers, and if workers are an essential input to recruiting, it might be argued that the firm can never successfully hire a worker. Since I will be thinking of the time period of the model as a quarter or a year, this assumption should be seen as a convenient way of representing the equilibrium of a dynamic process. The firm puts forward a plan that consists of a feasible 4-tuple $\{V, Y, L, X\}$. Given the exogenous hiring elasticity, q, a plan to use V workers in recruiting results in qV workers employed, of whom X are used to produce commodities.

Solving the firm's problem leads to the correspondence

$$V = \begin{cases} \infty & \text{if } \left(pA\left(1 - \frac{1}{q}\right) - w\right) > 0, \\ [0, \infty] & \text{if } \left(pA\left(1 - \frac{1}{q}\right) - w\right) = 0, \\ 0 & \text{if } \left(pA\left(1 - \frac{1}{q}\right) - w\right) < 0. \end{cases} \tag{2.14}$$

This expression is closely related to the condition that would arise in a model where labor is hired in a spot market. In a model of that kind, there is no need for a recruiting department and one would require the real wage, w/p, to equal the marginal product of labor,

$$A = \frac{w}{p},\tag{2.15}$$

in order for the firm to produce positive output. If productivity, A, were greater than w/p, the firm would be willing to expand without limit. If A were less than the real wage, the firm would shut down.

The correspondence represented in Equation (2.14) is similar to the labor demand correspondence that holds when labor is hired in a spot market but productivity is weighted by the hiring effectiveness parameter, q, which represents the number of workers that can be hired by a single recruiter.[5] As this parameter gets large, the relative size of the recruiting department shrinks. In the limit, as $q \to \infty$, the production function of the search model converges to that of the spot market model. The technology of the spot market model delivers a restriction on the real wage in equilibrium in the form of Equation (2.15). The search market equivalent is the equation

$$A\left(1 - \frac{1}{q}\right) = \frac{w}{p}.\tag{2.16}$$

Equation (2.16) is consistent with a range of equilibrium real wages since the hiring effectiveness parameter, q, is an endogenous variable. Existence of a solution with nonzero output requires $q > 1$. If q is large, a small recruiting department can support a large workforce and productivity, and the real wage, will be high in a zero profit equilibrium. If q is small, the reverse is true and in the limit, as q approaches 1, the entire workforce is engaged in recruiting and there is no one left to produce commodities.

2.1.4 SEARCH AND THE LABOR MARKET

The structure of the labor market in this model is similar to other search models. It differs in the assumption that firms must all offer the same wage and that this wage is determined in advance. There are many alternative assumptions that one might make about the structure of a labor market in which there are search frictions. For example, firms and workers might bargain over the wage after a match is formed, as in the random search model of Mortensen and Pissarides (1994), or they might influence the number of workers that take jobs, as in models of directed search. For a complete discussion of alternative models, see the survey article by Richard Rogerson, Robert Shimer, and Randall Wright (2005). The assumption that I am making is closest to the competitive search model of Espen Moen (1997) and Shimer (1996), which combines wage posting with directed search.

In a standard model of competitive search equilibrium, one conceives of there being many submarkets for labor—each directed by a market maker. Submarkets are distinguished by the wage that a firm will pay to a worker if the pair is matched. Conceptually, these submarkets might represent different geographical areas or different occupational categories. In the limiting case that I consider here, firms and workers are identical and can move costlessly between submarkets. Moen shows that competition between market makers will lead to an equilibrium in which market makers charge a zero entry fee, firms earn zero profits, and the workers' utility is maximized: This equilibrium implements a planning optimum.

Although I use the competitive search framework, I explore the polar opposite assumption to that of frictionless search markets. I assume that there are no competitive market makers and the wage does not adjust to implement the planning optimum. As a consequence of this assumption, there are many search equilibria, each of which can be Pareto ranked. I see this as a realistic way of capturing the idea that an economy may become stuck in a situation in which the social equilibrium is suboptimal but in which no individual agent can profit from taking a different action.

To implement a search equilibrium, I assume the existence of an aggregate match technology. The match technology takes the form,

$$\bar{m} = \bar{H}^{1/2} \bar{V}^{1/2}, \tag{2.17}$$

where $\bar{m}$ is the measure of workers that find jobs when $\bar{H}$ unemployed workers search and a measure $\bar{V}$ of workers are assigned to post vacancies by firms. I have used bars over variables to distinguish aggregate from individual values. Since $\bar{H} = 1$, this equation simplifies as follows,

$$\bar{m} = \bar{V}^{1/2}. \tag{2.18}$$

A further simplification follows from the fact that, since all workers are initially unemployed, employment and matches are the same thing and hence,[6]

$$\bar{L} = \bar{V}^{1/2}.$$ (2.19)

In all remaining models in this book, I suppress the notation for H since I maintain the assumptions that there is a unit measure of searching workers and that leisure does not yield disutility.

2.2 *Equilibrium and the Social Planner*

In Section 2.3, I define an equilibrium concept that captures the idea of effective demand. Before taking this step, it is helpful to have a benchmark against which to measure the properties of equilibrium.

2.2.1 THE PLANNING PROBLEM

Consider a benevolent social planner who maximizes the welfare of the representative family. The planner solves the problem

$$\max_{\{C,V,L\}} J = j(C)$$ (2.20)

$$C \leq AX,$$ (2.21)

$$L = X + V,$$ (2.22)

$$L = V^{1/2},$$ (2.23)

$$L + U = 1.$$ (2.24)

Since the objective function is increasing in C, the inequality (2.21) will hold with equality. Using this fact and combining equations (2.21) through (2.23) leads to the expression

$$C = AL(1 - L),$$ (2.25)

which is maximized at

$$V^* = \frac{1}{4}, \quad L^* = \frac{1}{2}, \quad C^* = \frac{A}{4}.$$ (2.26)

Figure 2.1 illustrates the nature of this solution on a graph.[7] Since there is a representative family in this economy, the only effective

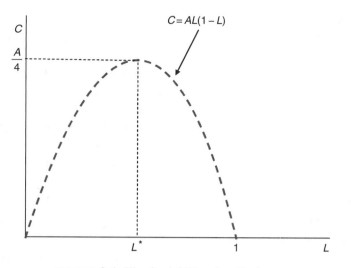

FIGURE 2.1 The Social Planning Optimum

decision of the social planner is how many workers to allocate to recruiting. Given the search technology, the optimum is achieved at $V^* = 1/4$. Any additional allocation of workers to recruiting would be counterproductive. Although the social planner could increase employment, the additional employed workers would not produce additional output—they would simply be recruiting additional recruiters and the resulting allocation would leave less, not more, output available for consumption.

The social planning solution provides a clear candidate definition of full employment—it is the level of employment L^* that maximizes per capita output. In *The General Theory*, Keynes argued that a laissez faire economic system would not necessarily achieve full employment, and he claimed the possibility of equilibria at less than full employment as a consequence of what he called a failure of effective demand. Section 2.3 makes this notion precise in a microfounded model based on labor market search.

2.2.2 AGGREGATE DEMAND AND SUPPLY

Before giving a formal definition of equilibrium, I will outline Keynes's principle of effective demand in the context of a one-good general equilibrium model where the spot market model of the labor market is replaced by an appropriate definition of search market equilibrium.

Keynes defined the *aggregate supply price* of a given volume of employment to be the

expectation of proceeds which will just make it worth the while of the entrepreneurs to give that employment. (Keynes, 1936, p. 24)

In Chapter 3, I provide a multisector version of the model. This definition easily generalizes to that case. In the one-sector representative agent version, the following simplifications are possible. First, if one assumes rational expectations and no uncertainty, then "expectations of proceeds" may be replaced by "proceeds." Second, proceeds are defined as factor cost plus profits and, in the representative agent environment, this is equivalent to the value of nominal GDP. Third, since I will be concerned with a real model, nominal and real GDP can be set equal to each other by choosing an appropriate numeraire.

It is tempting to notice that, in the one-good model, it is possible to choose a price normalization rule by setting $p = 1$. I will resist this normalization since it does not generalize to the multiple-good world and instead I will choose the normalization $w = 1$. This implies that p is the inverse of the real wage. This fact is important in interpreting the aggregate supply and demand diagram of *The General Theory*.

The Keynesian aggregate supply function may be represented on a diagram that measures the aggregate supply price in units of money on the vertical axis, which Keynes called Z, and ordinary units of labor on the horizontal axis, which Keynes called N. I have replaced the N of *The General Theory* with the symbol L to be consistent with the notation introduced earlier in the chapter. Using this notational change, one can write Keynes's *Aggregate Supply Function* as

$$Z = \phi(L). \tag{2.27}$$

Bear in mind that in *The General Theory*, Z is the value of a set of heterogenous commodities, and it is only in the one-commodity model that it can be reduced to the expression

$$Z \equiv pY, \tag{2.28}$$

where Y is the number of physical units of the produced good. More generally, Z would be defined by the expression

$$Z \equiv \sum_{i=1}^{n} p_i Y_i. \tag{2.29}$$

To complete the description of his equilibrium concept, Keynes defined D to be

> the proceeds which entrepreneurs expect to receive from the employment of L men, the relationship between D and L being written $D = f(L)$ which can be called the *Aggregate Demand Function*. (Keynes, 1936, p. 25; "L" is substituted for "N" from the original)

Like Z, D is measured in monetary units. Keynes's *principle of effective demand* amounts to the propositions that (1) employment is determined by the intersection of the aggregate demand and supply schedules and (2) equilibrium may occur at a point less than L^*, the full employment level that I have defined as the solution to the social planning problem.

To elucidate the properties of aggregate supply, Keynes asked us to consider what would happen if, for a given value of employment, aggregate demand D is greater than aggregate supply Z. In that case,..

> there will be an incentive to entrepreneurs to increase employment beyond L and, if necessary, *to raise costs by competing with one another for the factors of production*, up to the value of L for which Z has become equal to D. (Keynes, 1936, p. 25; "N" replaced by "L" and italics added)

In the one-good representative agent model, the principle of effective demand implies that competition between profit-maximizing firms will cause the real wage to adjust to the point where profit is equal to zero. The following algebra establishes that for values of D in a given interval, there will exist a real wage that has this property.

Consider the implications of assuming that the economy is in a symmetric equilibrium in which firms take the hiring effectiveness parameter, q, as given. Symmetry implies that the variables V and $\bar{V}$ and L and $\bar{L}$ are equal, and the assumption that firms take q parametrically implies

$$L = qV. \tag{2.30}$$

From the properties of the aggregate technology,

$$\bar{L} = \bar{V}^{1/2}. \tag{2.31}$$

It follows, in a symmetric equilibrium, that the following expressions characterize the relationships between q, V, and L:

$$q = \frac{1}{L}, \quad V = L^2. \tag{2.32}$$

Combining the first of these expressions with the first order profit maximizing condition, Equation (2.16), it follows that there exists an equilibrium for any value of $L \in [0, 1]$ with a real wage, given by the expression

$$\frac{w}{p} = A(1 - L), \tag{2.33}$$

which, given the normalization $w = 1$, implies

$$p = \frac{1}{A(1 - L)}. \tag{2.34}$$

Since the private technology is linear, firms make zero profit in equilibrium. One can combine Equations (2.11), (2.12), and (2.32) to yield the following expression for the physical quantity of output produced in this economy:

$$Y = AL(1 - L) \equiv \psi(L). \tag{2.35}$$

Combining Equations (2.34) and (2.35) leads to the following expression for aggregate supply:

$$Z = pY = L. \tag{2.36}$$

The aggregate supply function, $\phi(L)$, and the output function, $Y = \psi(L)$, are graphed on Figure 2.2 as the solid line and the dashed curve.[8] Moving along the aggregate supply function from zero to L^*, output is increasing. Moving beyond L^*, aggregate supply as defined by Keynes continues to increase as the price level rises, but the physical quantity of the produced good falls. Although it is tempting to refer to $\psi(L)$ as the aggregate supply function, this would be a mistake since, as Keynes made clear in *The General Theory*, this measure cannot easily be generalized beyond the one-good case.

2.2.3 EFFECTIVE DEMAND AND THE MULTIPLIER

In modern Dynamic Stochastic General Equilibrium (DSGE) models, the government is assumed to choose expenditure and taxes subject to a constraint. Models that incorporate a constraint of this kind were dubbed Ricardian by Robert Barro (1974). But in models with multiple

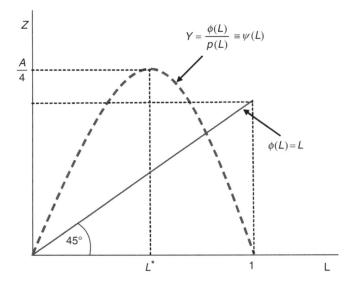

FIGURE 2.2 The Aggregate Supply Function

equilibria, there is no reason to impose a government budget constraint. When discussing models of monetary and fiscal policy, Eric Leeper (1991) has argued that one should allow government to choose both taxes and expenditure and that this choice selects an equilibrium. He calls a policy in which the government chooses both taxes and expenditure an "active fiscal regime." The modified search model of the labor market is one with multiple equilibria, and hence, one can close the model in the way advocated by Leeper.

To derive the aggregate demand function for the one-good representative agent economy, one need only recognize that materials balance requires

$$D = pC. \tag{2.37}$$

This is the GDP accounting identity in a model with no government expenditure and no investment. Aggregate demand is related to employment by the expression

$$D = (1 - \tau)\, wL + TR, \tag{2.38}$$

where recall that τ is the tax rate and TR represents lump-sum transfers measured in dollars. Since we have chosen w as the numeraire, set equal to 1, it follows that aggregate demand is equal to

$$D = (1 - \tau)\, L + TR, \tag{2.39}$$

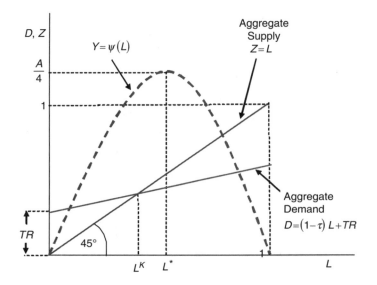

FIGURE 2.3 Aggregate Demand and Supply in the One-good Model

where all terms of this equation are now in wage units. Recall, from Equation (2.36), that aggregate supply is given by the expression

$$Z = L. \tag{2.40}$$

Substituting (2.40) into (2.39), it follows that

$$D = (1 - \tau) Z + TR, \tag{2.41}$$

and that in equilibrium when $D = Z$, the equilibrium value of income, Z^K, is given by

$$Z^K = \frac{TR}{\tau}, \tag{2.42}$$

where the superscript K is for Keynesian. The aggregate supply function, Equation (2.36), and the aggregate demand function, Equation (2.39), are depicted in Figure 2.3 together with the physical quantity of output, Y.

The equilibrium depicted in Figure 2.3 is one where there is positive unemployment since L^K, the Keynesian equilibrium, is less than L^*, the social planning optimum. If government were to increase transfers, TR, it would be possible to increase the Keynesian equilibrium to a point to the right of L^*. A policy of this kind would result in a higher price level (a lower real wage), less output than at L^*, and overemployment, since the Keynesian equilibrium would be associated with too many workers employed.

2.3 A Formal Definition of Equilibrium

This section provides a formal definition of equilibrium based on the ideas outlined earlier. I appropriate a term, *demand-constrained equilibrium*, from literature developed in the 1970s by Jean Pascal Benassy (1975), Jacques Dreze (1975), and Edmond Malinvaud (1977). Although fixed-price models with rationing of the kind studied by these authors are sometimes called demand-constrained equilibria, that is not what I mean here. Instead, I use this term to refer to a competitive search model that is closed with a materials balance condition. The common heritage of both usages of demand-constrained equilibrium is the idea of effective demand from Keynes's *General Theory*.

> *Definition 2.1:* (Demand-Constrained Equilibrium): For any given τ and TR, a symmetric demand-constrained equilibrium (DCE) is a real wage w/p, an allocation $\{Y, C, V, L, X\}$, and a pair of numbers $\tilde{q}$ and q, with the following properties:

(1) Feasibility:

$$Y \leq AX, \tag{2.43}$$

$$C \leq Y, \tag{2.44}$$

$$L \leq V^{1/2}, \tag{2.45}$$

$$X + V = L, \tag{2.46}$$

$$\frac{TR}{w} \leq \tau \frac{p}{w} AX. \tag{2.47}$$

(2) Consistency with optimal choices by firms and households:

$$V = \begin{cases} \infty & \text{if } \left(A\left(1 - \frac{1}{q}\right) - \frac{w}{p}\right) > 0, \\ [0, \infty] & \text{if } \left(A\left(1 - \frac{1}{q}\right) - \frac{w}{p}\right) = 0, \\ 0 & \text{if } \left(A\left(1 - \frac{1}{q}\right) - \frac{w}{p}\right) < 0, \end{cases} \tag{2.48}$$

$$\frac{p}{w}C = L(1-\tau) + \frac{TR}{w}. \tag{2.49}$$

(3) Search market equilibrium:

$$\tilde{q} = L \tag{2.50}$$

$$q = \frac{L}{V}. \tag{2.51}$$

The modified search model of the labor market provides a microfoundation to the "Keynesian cross" that characterized textbook descriptions of Keynesian economics in the 1960s. Income, equal to output, is demand determined and equal to a multiple of exogenous expenditure. Since I have abstracted from saving and investment, aggregate expenditure is determined as a multiple of transfer payments, where the multiplier is the inverse of the tax rate.

2.4 Concluding Comments

The model I have described has many features in common with the "Keynesian cross" that was taught to several generations of undergraduates. That model was criticized by Patinkin (1956), among others, since it lacked a coherent theory of the labor market. Patinkin combined Keynesian economics with general equilibrium theory by including the real value of money balances in utility and production functions. Although this route was intellectually coherent, it castrated the main message of *The General Theory*: that the level of economic activity is demand determined *in equilibrium*.[9]

A major criticism of Keynesian theory is that, when augmented by a classical model of the labor market, unemployed workers are given an incentive to offer to work for a lower wage. The combination of a complete set of Walrasian markets and a demand-determined level of economic activity is inconsistent: It results in a system with one more equation than unknown. The search-based model of the labor market described in this chapter provides a microfoundation to Keynesian economics that is not Walrasian since by assumption, agents do not trade the inputs to the search technology in competitive markets. The search technology has two inputs: unemployed workers and vacancies and a single price, the real wage. The resulting model lacks one equilibrium condition, which makes it a perfect partner for the Keynesian theory of demand determination. The resulting synthesis leads to a coherent theory of output and relative prices that does not suffer from the classical criticism that unemployed workers have an incentive to offer to work for a lower wage.

CHAPTER 3 | An Extension to Multiple Goods

T HE CONCEPTS OF AGGREGATE demand and supply are widely used
by contemporary economists.[10] My purpose in this chapter is to
explain the meaning that Keynes gave to them. Aggregate demand and
supply are typically explained in the context of a one-commodity model
in which real GDP is unambiguously measured in units of commodities
per unit of time. In *The General Theory*, there is no assumption that the
world can be described by a single-commodity model.

Chapter 4 of *The General Theory* is devoted to the choice of units.
Here, Keynes is clear that he will use only two units of measurement,
a monetary unit (I will call this a dollar) and a unit of ordinary labor.
The theory of index numbers was not as well developed as it is today,
and Keynes's use of these units to describe relationships among the
components of aggregate economic activity was clever and new.

Keynes chose "an hour's unit of ordinary labor" to represent the level
of economic activity because it is a relatively homogeneous unit. To get
around the fact that different workers have different skills, he proposed
to measure labor of different efficiencies by relative wages. Thus,

... the quantity of employment can be sufficiently defined for our
purpose by taking an hour's employment of ordinary labour as
our unit and weighting an hour's employment of special labor in
proportion to its remuneration; i.e. an hour of special labour remu-
nerated at double ordinary rates will count as two units. (Keynes,
1936, p. 41)

The other unit that Keynes uses in *The General Theory* is that of monetary value. His aggregate demand and supply curves are relationships between the value of aggregate GDP measured in dollars and the volume of aggregate employment measured in units of ordinary labor. This is not the same as the relationship between a price index and a quantity index that is used to explain aggregate demand and supply in most modern textbooks.

3.1 The Structure of the Model

This section extends the model of Chapter 2 by adding multiple goods. I will begin by describing the problem of the households.

3.1.1 HOUSEHOLDS

Since I am going to concentrate on the theory of aggregate supply, I will continue to assume the existence of identical households, each of which solves the problem

$$\max_{\{C\}} J = j\,(\mathbf{C})\,, \tag{3.1}$$

$$\mathbf{p} \cdot \mathbf{C} \le (1 - \tau)\left(Lw + \mathbf{r} \cdot \bar{\mathbf{K}}\right) + TR, \tag{3.2}$$

$$L = \tilde{q}, \tag{3.3}$$

$$U = 1 - L. \tag{3.4}$$

Each household has a measure 1 of members. $\mathbf{C}$ is a vector of n commodities, $\mathbf{p}$ is a vector of n money prices, w is the money wage, $\mathbf{r}$ is a vector of money rental rates, and $\bar{\mathbf{K}}$ is a vector of m factor endowments. I use the symbol r_j to refer to the jth rental rate. The factors may be thought of as different types of land. I will maintain the convention throughout the book that boldface letters are vectors and $\mathbf{x} \cdot \mathbf{y}$ is a vector product.

The household sends a measure 1 of members to search for jobs. Of these workers, $\tilde{q}$ find jobs and the household distributes the income of the employed workers across all family members. The household chooses to allocate its income to each of the n commodities. *TR* is the lump-sum household transfer (measured in dollars) and τ the income-tax rate. The employment rate $\tilde{q}$ is taken parametrically by households. I will assume that utility takes the form

$$j(\mathbf{C}) = \sum_{i=1}^{n} g_i \log(C_i),$$ (3.5)

where the utility weights sum to 1,

$$\sum_{i=1}^{n} g_i = 1.$$ (3.6)

Later, I will also assume that each good is produced by a Cobb-Douglas production function and I will refer to the resulting model as a logarithmic Cobb-Douglas, or LCD, economy. Although the analysis could be generalized to allow utility to be homothetic and technologies to be Constant Elasticity of Substitution (CES), this extension would considerably complicate the algebra. My intent is to find a compromise model that allows for multiple commodities but is still tractable, and for this purpose, the log utility model is familiar and suitable.

The solution to the utility maximization problem has the form

$$p_i C_i = g_i Z^D,$$ (3.7)

where g_i is the budget share allocated to the ith good. For more general homothetic preferences, these shares would be functions of the price vector $\mathbf{p}$. Household income, Z, is defined as

$$Z \equiv Lw + \mathbf{r} \cdot \bar{\mathbf{K}},$$ (3.8)

and is measured in dollars. The term Z^D in Equation (3.7) represents disposable income and is defined by the equation

$$Z^D = (1 - \tau) Z + TR.$$ (3.9)

Since all income is derived from the production of commodities, it follows from the aggregate budget constraints of households, firms, and government that Z is also equal to the value of the produced commodities in the economy,

$$Z \equiv \sum_{i=1}^{n} p_i Y_i.$$ (3.10)

The equivalence of income and the value of output is a restatement of the familiar Keynesian accounting identity, immortalized in the textbook concept of the "circular flow of income."

3.1.2 FIRMS

There are $n \geq m$ commodities. Output of the ith commodity is denoted Y_i, and is produced by a constant returns-to-scale production function,

$$Y_i = \Psi_i \left(\mathbf{K}_i, X_i \right), \tag{3.11}$$

where $\mathbf{K}_i$ is a vector of m capital goods used in the ith industry and X_i is labor used in production in industry i. The jth element of $\mathbf{K}_i$, denoted $K_{i,j}$, is the measure of the jth capital good used as an input to the ith industry and $\mathbf{K}_i$ is defined as

$$\mathbf{K}_i \equiv \left(K_{i,1}, K_{i,2} \ldots, K_{i,m} \right). \tag{3.12}$$

The function Ψ_i is assumed to be Cobb-Douglas,

$$\Psi_i \left(\mathbf{K}_i, X_i \right) \equiv A_i K_{i,1}^{a_{i,1}} K_{i,2}^{a_{i,2}} \ldots K_{i,m}^{a_{i,m}} X_i^{b_i}, \tag{3.13}$$

where the constant returns-to-scale assumption implies that the weights $a_{i,j}$ and b_i sum to 1,

$$\sum_{j=1}^{m} a_{i,j} + b_i = 1. \tag{3.14}$$

Since the assumption of constant returns to scale implies that the number of firms in each industry is indeterminate, I will refer interchangeably to Y_i as the output of a firm or of an industry.

Each firm recruits workers in a search market by allocating a measure V_i of workers to recruiting. The total measure of workers, L_i, employed in industry, i, is

$$L_i = X_i + V_i. \tag{3.15}$$

Each firm takes parametrically the measure of workers that can be hired, denoted q, and employment at firm i is related to V_i by the equation

$$L_i = q V_i. \tag{3.16}$$

The firm solves the problem

$$\max_{\{\mathbf{K}_i, V_i, X_i, L_i\}} p_i Y_i - w L_i - \mathbf{r} \cdot \mathbf{K}_i \tag{3.17}$$

$$Y_i \leq A_i K_{i,1}^{a_{i,1}} K_{i,2}^{a_{i,2}} \ldots K_{i,m}^{a_{i,m}} X_i^{b_i}, \tag{3.18}$$

$$L_i = X_i + V_i, \tag{3.19}$$

$$L_i = q V_i. \tag{3.20}$$

Using Equations (3.19) and (3.20), we can write labor used in production, X_i, as a multiple, Θ, of employment at the firm, L_i:

$$X_i = L_i \Theta, \tag{3.21}$$

where Θ is defined as

$$\Theta = \left(1 - \frac{1}{q}\right). \tag{3.22}$$

We may then write the problem in reduced form:

$$\max_{\{\mathbf{K}_i, V_i, X_i, L_i\}} p_i Y_i - w L_i - \mathbf{r} \cdot \mathbf{K}_i, \tag{3.23}$$

$$Y_i \leq A_i L_i^{b_i} \Theta^{b_i} K_{i,1}^{a_{i,1}} K_{i,2}^{a_{i,2}} \ldots K_{i,m}^{a_{i,m}}. \tag{3.24}$$

The solution to this problem is characterized by the first-order conditions

$$a_{i,j} p_i Y_i = K_{i,j} r_j, \quad j = 1, \ldots, m, \tag{3.25}$$

$$b_i p_i Y_i = w L_i. \tag{3.26}$$

Using these first-order conditions to write L_i and $K_{i,j}$ as functions of w, $\mathbf{r}$, and p_i and substituting these expressions into the production function leads to an expression for p_i in terms of factor prices,

$$p_i = p_i \left(\frac{w}{\Theta}, \mathbf{r}\right). \tag{3.27}$$

The function $p_i : R^{m+1} \to R_+$ is known as the factor price frontier and is homogenous of degree 1 in the vector of m money rental rates $\mathbf{r}$ and in the money wage, w.

3.1.3 SEARCH

I have described how individual households and firms respond to the aggregate variables w, $\mathbf{p}$, $\mathbf{r}$, q, and $\tilde{q}$. This section describes the process by which searching workers are allocated to jobs. I assume that there is an aggregate match technology of the form

$$\bar{m} = \bar{V}^{1/2}, \tag{3.28}$$

where $\bar{m}$ is the measure of workers that find jobs when a measure 1 of unemployed workers search and $\bar{V}$ workers are allocated to recruiting in aggregate by all firms. I have used bars over variables to distinguish aggregate from individual values. Further, since all workers are initially unemployed, employment and matches are equal,

$$\bar{L} = \bar{V}^{1/2}. \tag{3.29}$$

Jobs are allocated to the ith firm in proportion to the fraction of aggregate recruiters attached to firm i; that is,

$$L_i \equiv \bar{V}^{1/2} \frac{V_i}{\bar{V}}, \tag{3.30}$$

where V_i is the number of recruiters at firm i.

3.2 Equilibrium and the Social Planner

In this section, I extend the equilibrium concept from Chapter 2 to a multigood economy and I compare the properties of an equilibrium with the solution to a social planning solution in a multigood environment.

3.2.1 THE SOCIAL PLANNER

In the multigood economy, the planner solves the problem

$$\max_{\{C,V,L\}} j\,(\mathbf{C}) = \sum_{i=1}^{n} g_i \log{(C_i)} \tag{3.31}$$

$$C_i \leq A_i K_{i,1}^{a_{i,1}} K_{i,2}^{a_{i,2}} \dots K_{i,m}^{a_{i,m}} (L_i - V_i)^{b_i}, \quad i = 1, \dots n, \tag{3.32}$$

$$\sum_{i=1}^{n} K_{i,j} \leq \bar{K}_j, \quad j = 1, \dots m \tag{3.33}$$

$$L_i = \left(\frac{1}{\bar{V}}\right)^{1/2} V_i. \tag{3.34}$$

Equation (3.34) can be rearranged to give the following expression for aggregate employment as a function of aggregate labor devoted to recruiting:

$$\bar{L} \equiv \sum_{i=1}^{n} L_i = \bar{V}^{1/2}. \tag{3.35}$$

Combining this expression with Equation (3.34) leads to the following relationship between labor used in recruiting at firm i, employment at firm i, and aggregate employment:

$$V_i = L_i \bar{L}. \tag{3.36}$$

Equation (3.36) implies that it takes more effort on the part of the recruiting department of firm i to hire a new worker when aggregate employment is high; this is because of congestion effects in the matching process.

Using Equation (3.36) to eliminate V_i from the production function, we can rewrite (3.32) in terms of $\mathbf{K}_i$ and L_i:

$$C_i = A_i K_{i,1}^{a_{i,1}} K_{i,2}^{a_{i,2}} \dots K_{i,m}^{a_{i,m}} L_i^{b_i} \left(1 - \bar{L}\right)^{b_i}. \tag{3.37}$$

It follows that the externality Θ in Equation (3.24) is given by the expression

$$\Theta = \left(1 - \frac{1}{q}\right) = 1 - \bar{L}. \tag{3.38}$$

Equation (3.37) makes clear that the match technology leads to a production externality across firms. When all other firms have high levels of employment, it becomes harder for the individual firm to recruit workers and this shows up as an external productivity effect, which is the term $\left(1 - \bar{L}\right)$, in firm $i's$ production function. The externality is internalized by the social planner but may cause difficulties that private markets cannot effectively overcome. I will show that this externality is the source of Keynesian unemployment.

To find a solution to the social planning solution, we may substitute Equation (3.37) into the objective function (3.31) and exploit the logarithmic structure to write utility as a weighted sum of the logs of capital and labor used in each industry, and of the externality terms that depend on the log of $\left(1 - \bar{L}\right)$. The first-order conditions for the problem can then be written as

$$\frac{g_i b_i}{L_i} = \frac{\sum_{i=1}^{n} g_i b_i}{\left(1 - \bar{L}\right)}, \quad i = 1, \dots, n, \tag{3.39}$$

$$\frac{g_i a_{i,j}}{K_{i,j}} = \lambda_j, \quad i = 1, \dots, n, \quad j = 1, \dots, m, \tag{3.40}$$

$$\sum_{i=1}^{n} K_{i,j} = \bar{K}_j, \quad j = 1, \dots, m. \tag{3.41}$$

The variable λ_j is a Lagrange multiplier on the jth resource constraint. Using Equation (3.39) and the fact that $\bar{L} = \sum_{i=1}^{n} L_i$, it follows from some simple algebra that the social planner will make the same allocation of labor in the LCD economy as in the simple one-good model studied in Chapter 2:

$$\bar{L}^* = 1/2. \tag{3.42}$$

The first-order conditions can also be used to derive the following expression for the labor L_i^* used in industry i:

$$L_i^* = \frac{g_i b_i}{\sum_{i=1}^{n} g_i b_i} \bar{L}^*. \tag{3.43}$$

To derive the capital allocation across firms for capital good j, the social planner solves Equations (3.40) and (3.41) to yield the optimal allocation of capital good j to industry i:

$$K_{i,j}^* = \frac{g_i a_{i,j}}{\sum_{i=1}^{n} g_i a_{i,j}} \bar{K}_j. \tag{3.44}$$

For the LCD economy, the social planner sets employment at $1/2$ and allocates factors across industries using weights that depend on a combination of factor shares and preference weights.[11]

3.2.2 AGGREGATE DEMAND AND SUPPLY

This section derives the properties of the Keynesian aggregate supply curve for the LCD economy. When I began this project, I thought of aggregate supply as a relationship between employment and output. Intuition that was carried over from my own undergraduate training led me to think of this function as analogous to a movement along a production function in a one-good economy. This intuition is incorrect. A more appropriate analogy would be to compare the aggregate supply function to the first-order condition for labor in a one-good model.

Consider a one-good economy in which output, Y, is produced from labor, L, and capital, K, using the function

$$Y = A\left(\bar{L}\right) K^{\alpha} L^{1-\alpha}, \tag{3.45}$$

where A may be a function of aggregate employment because of the search externalities discussed earlier. It would be a mistake to call the function

$$A\left(L\right) K^{\alpha} L^{1-\alpha}, \tag{3.46}$$

where $\bar{L}$ is replaced by L, the Keynesian aggregate supply function.

In the one-good economy, the equation that triggers competition for workers is the first-order condition

$$\frac{(1-\alpha)\,Y}{L} = \frac{w}{p}.$$ (3.47)

Aggregate supply, Z, is price times quantity. Using this definition, Equation (3.47) can be rearranged to yield the expression

$$Z \equiv pY = \frac{wL}{(1-\alpha)},$$ (3.48)

which is the Keynesian aggregate supply function. By fixing the money wage, Keynes was not assuming disequilibrium in factor markets; he was choosing a numeraire. Once this is recognized, the Keynesian aggregate supply curve takes on a different interpretation from that which is given in introductory textbooks. A movement along the aggregate supply curve is associated with an increase in the price level that reduces the real wage and brings it into equality with a falling marginal product of labor.

In an economy with many goods, the aggregate supply price, Z, is defined by the expression

$$Z \equiv \sum_{i=1}^{n} p_i Y_i.$$ (3.49)

For the LCD economy, the aggregate supply function has a particularly simple form since the logarithmic and Cobb-Douglas functional forms allow individual demands and supplies to be aggregated. The first-order condition for the use of labor at firm i has the form

$$L_i = \frac{b_i Y_i p_i}{w}.$$ (3.50)

To aggregate labor across industries, we need to know how relative prices adjust as the economy expands. To determine relative prices, we must turn to preferences and here the assumption of logarithmic utility allows a simplification since the representative agent consumes the output of every industry and allocates fixed budget shares to each commodity:

$$Y_i p_i = C_i p_i = g_i Z^D,$$ (3.51)

where Z^D is disposable income. Combining Equation (3.50) with (3.51) yields the expression

$$L_i = \frac{b_i g_i Z^D}{w}.$$ (3.52)

Summing Equation (3.52) over all i industries and choosing $w = 1$ as the numeraire leads to the expression

$$Z^D = \frac{1}{\chi} L \equiv \phi(L),\qquad(3.53)$$

where

$$\chi \equiv \sum_{i=1}^{n} g_i b_i.\qquad(3.54)$$

Since the government budget must also balance,

$$TR = \tau Z,\qquad(3.55)$$

it follows that income and disposable income must be equal; that is,

$$Z^D = Z(1 - \tau) + TR = Z,\qquad(3.56)$$

and Equation (3.53) can be written as

$$Z = \frac{1}{\chi} L \equiv \phi(L).\qquad(3.57)$$

Equation (3.57) is the Keynesian aggregate supply curve for the multi-good logarithmic Cobb-Douglas economy. To reiterate, the aggregate supply curve in a one-good economy is not a production function. It is the first-order condition for labor. In the LCD economy, it is an aggregate of the first-order conditions across industries with a coefficient that is a weighted sum of preference and technology parameters for the different industries.

Can this expression be generalized beyond the LCD case? The answer is yes, but the resulting expression for aggregate supply depends, in general, on factor supplies; that is, Z will be a function not only of L but also of $\bar{K}_1, \ldots \bar{K}_m$. The following paragraph demonstrates that, given our special assumptions about preferences and technologies, these stocks serve only to influence rental rates.

The first-order condition for the jth factor used in firm i can be written as

$$K_{i,j} = \frac{a_{i,j} Y_i p_i}{r_j}.\qquad(3.58)$$

Combining the first-order conditions for factor j and summing over all i industries leads to the expression

$$\bar{K}_j = \sum_{i=1}^{n} K_{i,j} = \frac{\sum_{i=1}^{n} a_{i,j} Y_i p_i}{r_j}.\qquad(3.59)$$

Exploiting the allocation of budget shares by consumers, Equation (3.51), one can derive the following expression:

$$r_j = \frac{\psi_j Z}{\bar{K}_j},$$ (3.60)

where

$$\psi_j \equiv \sum_{i=1}^{n} a_{i,j} g_i.$$ (3.61)

Equation (3.60) determines the nominal rental rate for factor j as a function of the aggregate supply price, Z, and the factor supply, $\bar{K}_j$.

3.2.3 KEYNESIAN EQUILIBRIUM

What determines relative outputs in the Keynesian model and how are aggregate employment, L, and the aggregate supply price, Z, determined? As in the one-good model, aggregate demand follows from the GDP accounting identity,

$$D = \sum_{i=1}^{n} p_i C_i.$$ (3.62)

In an economy with government purchases and investment expenditure, this equation would have two extra terms as in the textbook Keynesian accounting identity that generations of students have written as

$$Y = C + I + G.$$ (3.63)

In our notation, C is replaced by $\sum_{i=1}^{n} p_i C_i$, Y is replaced by D, and G and I are absent from the model. The Keynesian consumption function is simply the budget equation

$$\sum_{i=1}^{n} p_i C_i = (1 - \tau) Z + TR,$$ (3.64)

and since $D = \sum_{i=1}^{n} p_i C_i$ and $\chi Z = L$, from Equation (3.53), the aggregate demand function for the LCD economy is given by the equation

$$D = (1 - \tau) \frac{L}{\chi} + TR.$$ (3.65)

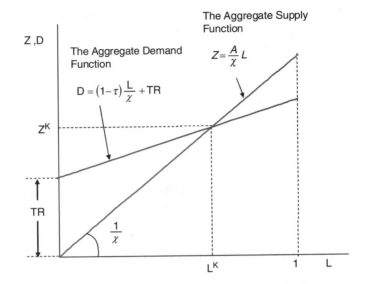

FIGURE 3.1 Aggregate Demand and Supply in the Multi-good Model

In a Keynesian equilibrium, when $D = Z$, the value of income, Z^K, is given by the equality of aggregate demand and supply; that is,

$$Z^K = \frac{TR}{\tau}, \tag{3.66}$$

and equilibrium employment is given by the expression

$$L^K = \chi Z^K.$$

The Keynesian aggregate demand and supply functions for the LCD economy are graphed in Figure 3.1.

3.3 Equilibrium and the Planning Optimum Compared

How well do markets work? Do we require government microman-agement of individual industries to correct inefficient allocations of resources that are inherent in capitalist economies? Keynes response to the first question was that the level of aggregate economic activity may be too low as a consequence of the failure of effective demand. For this reason, he was a strong proponent of government interven-tion. But Keynes's was not a communist and he recognized the merits of the free market as an allocation mechanism to distribute resources across industries. In this section, I will show that the model I have developed provides a formalization of Keynes's arguments. If effective demand is too low, the model displays an inefficient level of employment. In this sense there is an argument for a well-designed fiscal policy. But the allocation of factors across industries, for a given volume of employment, is the same allocation that would be achieved by a social planner. There is no reason for government to micromanage individual industries.

To make the argument for fiscal intervention, one need only compare aggregate employment in the social planning solution with aggregate employment in a Keynesian equilibrium. The social planner would choose

$$L^* = \frac{1}{2}. \tag{3.67}$$

The Keynesian equilibrium at

$$L^K = \frac{\chi TR}{\tau} \tag{3.68}$$

may result in any level of employment in the interval $[0, 1]$. For any value of $L^K < L^*$, we may say that the economy is experiencing Keynesian unemployment, and in this case there is a possible Pareto improvement that would make everyone better off by increasing the number of people employed.

The formalization of Keynesian economics based on search contains the additional implication that there may be overemployment as well as underemployment; that is, L^K may be greater than L^*. Overemployment is Pareto inefficient and welfare would be increased in an alternative equilibrium in which fewer workers were employed in every industry. Although a value of L^K greater than L^* is associated with a higher value of nominal GDP $(Z^K > Z^*)$, employment, in an equilibrium of this kind, is too high and the economy is not maximizing output measured in physical units. By lowering L back toward L^*, the economy can produce *more* goods in every industry. The increase in the physical quantity of each good is accompanied by an even greater drop in its price. This in turn causes the money value of output to fall even as the quantity produced of every good rises.

In an overemployment equilibrium, the additional workers spend more time recruiting their fellows than in productive activity. In the limit, as employment tends to 1, nominal GDP tends to its upper bound,

$1/\chi$. But although GDP measured in wage units always increases as employment increases, for very high values of employment the physical quantity of output produced in each industry is very low, and in the limit at $L = 1$, Y_i is equal to zero in each industry and p_i is infinite. Every employed worker is so busy recruiting additional workers that he or she has no time to produce commodities.

What about the allocation of factors across industries? Here, the capitalist system fares much better. Equations (3.43) and (3.44), which determine factor allocations in the social planning solution, are reproduced here:

$$L_i^* = \frac{g_i b_i}{\sum_{i=1}^{n} g_i b_i} L^*, \tag{3.69}$$

$$K_{i,j}^* = \frac{g_i a_{i,j}}{\sum_{i=1}^{n} g_i a_{i,j}} \bar{K}_j. \tag{3.70}$$

Given the resources $\bar{K}_j$ for $j = 1, ..., m$, Equation (3.70) implies that these resources will be allocated across industries in proportion to weights that depend on the preference parameters g_i and the production elasticities $a_{i,j}$. Equation (3.69) implies that the volume of resources employed, L^*, will be allocated across industries in a similar manner.

Contrast these equations with their counterparts for the Keynesian equilibrium. The factor demand equations (3.58) and the resource constraints (3.59) are reproduced here:

$$K_{i,j} = \frac{a_{i,j} Y_i p_i}{r_j}, \tag{3.71}$$

$$K_j = \sum_{i=1}^{n} K_{i,j} = \frac{\sum_{i=1}^{n} a_{i,j} Y_i p_i}{r_j}. \tag{3.72}$$

Consumers with logarithmic preferences will set budget shares to utility weights:

$$p_i Y_i = g_i Z. \tag{3.73}$$

Combining this expression with Equations (3.58) and (3.72) leads to the following equation, which determines the allocation of factor j to industry i in a Keynesian equilibrium:

$$K_{i,j} = \frac{g_i a_{i,j}}{\sum_{i=1}^{n} g_i a_{i,j}} \bar{K}_j. \tag{3.74}$$

This expression is identical to the social planning solution, Equation (3.70). In other words, capital is allocated efficiently across industries in a Keynesian equilibrium.

What about the allocation of labor across industries? The first-order conditions for firms imply

$$b_i p_i Y_i = w L_i. \tag{3.75}$$

Combining this expression with Equation (3.73) and using the fact that $\chi Z^K = L^K$ gives

$$L_i = \frac{g_i b_i}{\sum_{i=1}^{n} g_i b_i} L^K, \tag{3.76}$$

where I have used the fact that $\chi \equiv \sum_{i=1}^{n} g_i b_i$. Equation (3.76), which determines the allocation of labor across industries, is identical to the social planning solution with one exception; the efficient level of aggregate employment, L^*, is replaced by the Keynesian equilibrium level, L^K. It is in this sense that Keynes provided a *general* theory of employment. The classical value L^* is just one possible rest point of the capitalist system, as envisaged by Keynes, and in general it is not one that he thought would be found by unassisted competitive markets.

3.4 Concluding Comments

It is difficult to read *The General Theory* without experiencing a disconnect between what is in the book and what one has learned about Keynesian economics as a student. The most egregious misrepresentation is the notion of aggregate demand and supply that we teach to undergraduates and that bears little or no relationship to what Keynes meant by these terms. The representative textbook author has adopted the Humpty Dumpty approach that, "... when I use a word, it means just what I choose it to mean—neither more nor less."[12]

The textbook aggregate demand curve slopes down; the Keynesian aggregate demand curve slopes up. The textbook aggregate demand curve plots a price against a quantity; so does the Keynesian aggregate demand curve, at least in name, but the "aggregate demand price" and the "aggregate supply price" of *The General Theory* are very different animals from the price indices of modern theory. Beginning with Patinkin

(1956), textbook Keynesians have tried to fit the round peg of *The General Theory* into the square hole of Walrasian general equilibrium theory. The fact that the fit is less than perfect has caused several generations of students to abandon the ideas of *The General Theory* and to follow the theoretically more coherent approach of real business cycle theory. The time has come to reconsider this decision.

CHAPTER 4 | # A Model with Investment and Saving

THE MODELS I INTRODUCED in chapters 2 and 3 are missing a central component of *The General Theory*: the idea that investment is the driving force of business cycles. Chapter 4 introduces this idea by developing a model with saving and investment. In *The General Theory*, Keynes argued that the distinction between these concepts was central to his theory of effective demand. I will explain this distinction with a two-period model populated by three generations of households. One of these generations, the young in the first period, saves for the future and invests in capital to produce commodities in the second period. In Walrasian general equilibrium models, saving and investment are brought into equality by changes in intertemporal prices. In the Keynesian model, they are equated by changes in employment. Explaining the difference between these two mechanisms is the main purpose of this chapter.

Chapter 4 builds a model economy that has all the same features as the one-commodity environment that I introduced in Chapter 2. In addition, it has an extra period and a produced factor of production, capital. This richer structure allows me to discuss the idea that unemployment is produced by a lack of investment spending. Whereas effective demand in Chapter 2 was a function of fiscal policy, in this chapter it will also depend on the beliefs of investors.

4.1 The Model Structure and the Planning Solution

This section describes the physical environment and describes the social planning problem. There are two periods, labeled 1 and 2, and three generations, labeled 0, 1, and 2. In period 1, there are two generations alive. Generation 0 is old and owns the capital stock. Generation 1 is young and owns an endowment of time. At the end of period 1, generation 0 dies. At the beginning of period 2, generation 2 is born and is endowed with a production technology. Throughout the chapter, a superscript will index the period in which a generation was born and a subscript will index calendar time; thus, x_t^s is the date t value of the variable x associated with the generation born in period s.

4.1.1 HOUSEHOLDS

This section describes the economic choices made by households in each generation. I begin by describing the choices made by the old and the young in the first period; I refer to them as generations 0 and 1. I then move on to the second period of the model and introduce the choices of a third generation that I refer to as generation 2. The decisions of generations 0 and 2 are limited, and most of the action in this model takes place with the choices made by generation 1. One could develop the model by adding more periods and more generations, although I have not done that in this book.

The Initial Old

There are two coexistent generations in period 1. Generation 0 solves the problem

$$\max_{\{C_1^0\}} j^0\left(C_1^0\right),\tag{4.1}$$

subject to the constraint

$$p_1 C_1^0 \leq \left[(1-\delta)\, p_1 + r_1\right] K_1.\tag{4.2}$$

There is a unique commodity in each period that may be consumed or accumulated to be used as capital in production in the subsequent period. This commodity has money price p_1 in period 1. K_1 is an initial stock of capital owned by generation 0, r_1 is the money rental rate for capital in period 1, δ is the depreciation rate, and C_1^0 is consumption of generation 0 in period 1. Since I assume that the utility function $j^0\left(C_1^0\right)$ is increasing in C_1^0, the household's decision problem has the trivial solution

$$p_1 C_1^0 = \left[(1 - \delta)\, p_1 + r_1\right] K_1,\tag{4.3}$$

which directs the household to consume all of its wealth.[13]

The Initial Young

As in previous chapters, I assume a unit measure of households with preferences over current consumption of household members. The representative generation 1 household receives utility from consumption in periods 1 and 2 and solves the problem

$$\max_{\{C_1^1, C_2^1, K_2\}} j^1\left(C_1^1, C_2^1\right) = g_1 \log\left(C_1^1\right) + g_2 \log\left(C_2^1\right),\tag{4.4}$$

where the preference weights g_1 and g_2 sum to 1:

$$g_1 + g_2 = 1.\tag{4.5}$$

Each household member is endowed with a single unit of time in period 1 and a unit measure of household members searches for a job. Of these workers, a fraction L_1 find a job and the remaining U_1 are unemployed; hence,

$$L_1 + U_1 = 1.\tag{4.6}$$

In a search equilibrium, a fraction $\tilde{q}$ workers find a job and L_1 is given by the expression

$$L_1 = \tilde{q},\tag{4.7}$$

where $\tilde{q}$ is taken parametrically by the household.

Generation 1's allocation problem is subject to the sequence of budget constraints

$$p_1 C_1^1 + p_1 K_2 \le w_1 L_1,\tag{4.8}$$

$$p_2 C_2^1 \le (r_2 + p_2 (1 - \delta)) K_2,\tag{4.9}$$

where w_1 is the money wage in period 1, K_2 is capital carried into period 2, r_2 is the money rental rate in period 2, and p_2 is the money price in period 2. Households may borrow and lend with each other at money interest rate i, and hence the intertemporal budget constraint is

$$p_1 C_1^1 + \frac{p_2}{1+i} C_2^1 \le w_1 L_1.\tag{4.10}$$

The solution to this problem is characterized by the consumption allocation decisions,

$$p_1 C_1^1 = g_1 w_1 L_1, \qquad (4.11)$$

$$\frac{p_2 C_2^1}{1+i} = g_2 w_1 L_1, \qquad (4.12)$$

and the no-arbitrage condition,

$$1 + i = \left(\frac{r_2}{p_2} + 1 - \delta \right) \frac{p_2}{p_1}, \qquad (4.13)$$

that defines the money interest rate i at which households have no desire
to borrow or lend with each other.

The Third Generation

In period 2, there is a third generation that solves the problem

$$\max_{\{K_2, C_2^2\}} j^2 \left(C_2^2 \right), \qquad (4.14)$$

$$p_2 C_2^2 \le p_2 Y_2 - r_2 K_2, \qquad (4.15)$$

where output Y_2 is produced with the technology

$$Y_2 \le K_2^\alpha. \qquad (4.16)$$

The solution to this problem is given by the expression

$$C_2^2 = Y_2 - \frac{r_2}{p_2} K_2. \qquad (4.17)$$

In a model of multiple generations, each generation would face a
problem like that of generation 1. To keep this two-period example as
simple as possible, I assume here that generation 2 owns the technology
described by Equation (4.16) and that members of this generation rent
capital from generation 1 and produce output Y_2. There is no labor market
in period 2.

4.1.2 FIRMS

I have described the decisions made by households, and I have also
explained production in period 2. This section describes the choices made
by firms in period 1. Since the structure of this problem is a special case
of the problem described in Chapter 3, I will be relatively brief in my
description.

There is a large number of competitive firms, each of which solves the problem

$$\max_{\{Y_1, K_1, V_1, L_1, X_1\}} p_1 Y_1 - w_1 L_1 - r_1 K_1, \tag{4.18}$$

subject to the constraints

$$Y_1 \leq A K_1^\alpha X_1^{1-\alpha}, \tag{4.19}$$

$$L_1 = X_1 + V_1, \tag{4.20}$$

$$L_1 = q V_1. \tag{4.21}$$

As in chapters 2 and 3, the firm must choose a feasible plan $\{Y_1, K_1, V_1, L_1, X_1\}$ to maximize profit, taking the wage w_1, the rental rate r_1, the price p_1, and the recruiting efficiency q as given. A firm that allocates V_1 workers to recruiting will hire $q V_1 = L_1$ workers, of which X_1 will be allocated to productive activity.

The solution to this problem is characterized by the first-order conditions

$$(1 - \alpha) \frac{Y_1}{L_1} = \frac{w_1}{p_1}, \tag{4.22}$$

$$\alpha \frac{Y_1}{K_1} = \frac{r_1}{p_1}, \tag{4.23}$$

and the factor price frontier

$$p_1 = \frac{1}{A} \left(\frac{w_1}{[1 - \alpha] \Theta} \right)^{1-\alpha} \left(\frac{r_1}{\alpha} \right)^\alpha, \tag{4.24}$$

where the aggregate productivity variable

$$\Theta = \left(1 - \frac{1}{q} \right) \tag{4.25}$$

is taken as given by the individual firm.

4.1.3 SEARCH

The search technology is identical to that described in Chapter 2. There is a match technology of the form

$$\bar{L}_1 = \bar{V}_1^{1/2}, \tag{4.26}$$

where $\bar{L}$ is employment, equal to the measure of workers that find jobs when a unit measure of unemployed workers search and $\bar{V}_1$ workers are allocated to recruiting by firms.

In a symmetric equilibrium, equations (4.20), (4.21), and (4.26) imply

$$\Theta = \left(1 - \bar{L}_1\right). \tag{4.27}$$

4.1.4 THE SOCIAL PLANNER

How would a benevolent social planner arrange production and consumption in this economy? This section addresses that question by studying the solution to the following constrained optimization problem:

$$\max_{\{K_2, L_1, C_1^0, C_1^1, C_2^1\}} \lambda_0 j^0\left(C_1^0\right) + \lambda_1 j^1\left(C_1^1, C_2^1\right) + \lambda_2 j^2\left(C_2^2\right), \tag{4.28}$$

$$C_1^0 + C_1^1 + K_2 \le A K_1^\alpha L_1^{1-\alpha} \left(1 - L_1\right)^{1-\alpha} + K_1 \left(1 - \delta\right), \tag{4.29}$$

$$C_2^1 + C_2^2 \le K_2^\alpha + \left(1 - \delta\right) K_2, \tag{4.30}$$

where the numbers λ_i are welfare weights that sum to 1:

$$\lambda_1 + \lambda_2 + \lambda_3 = 1. \tag{4.31}$$

The social planner chooses K_2, the amount of capital to carry into period 2; L_1, employment in period 1; and a way of allocating commodities to individuals, $\{C_1^0, C_1^1, C_2^1, C_2^2\}$. His or her problem is characterized as the maximization of Equation (4.28) subject to the two feasibility constraints (4.29) and (4.30).

The solution to this problem requires that the two inequalities (4.29) and (4.30) should hold with equality and, in addition, the following six first-order conditions should be satisfied:

$$-\mu_1 + \mu_2 \alpha K_2^{\alpha-1} = 0, \tag{4.32}$$

$$(1 - \alpha) A K_1^\alpha L_1^{1-\alpha} \left(1 - L_1\right)^{1-\alpha} \left(\frac{1}{L_1} - \frac{1}{1 - L_1}\right) = 0, \tag{4.33}$$

$$\lambda_0 j_1^0\left(C_1^0\right) = \mu_1, \tag{4.34}$$

$$\lambda_1 j_1^1\left(C_1^1, C_2^1\right) = \mu_1, \tag{4.35}$$

$$\lambda_1 j_2^1\left(C_1^1, C_2^1\right) = \mu_2, \tag{4.36}$$

$$\lambda_2 j_1^2\left(C_2^2\right) = \mu_2. \tag{4.37}$$

The six equations (4.32) through (4.37) and the two constraints (4.29) and (4.30) determine the six variables K_2, L_1, C_1^0, C_1^1, C_2^1, and C_2^2 and the two Lagrange multipliers μ_1 and μ_2 associated with the inequality constraints (4.29) and (4.30).

The most important of these conditions is Equation (4.33), which implies that optimal employment in period 1, call this L_1^*, occurs when

$$L_1^* = \frac{1}{2}. \tag{4.38}$$

This problem differs from a conventional social planning problem since there is an externality in the technology that is internalized by the social planner. This is the occurrence of the term $1 - L_1$ in the production function in period 1. In all other ways, the problem is conventional. Given L_1, the planner chooses how to allocate commodities across individuals and across time. I show later that the existence of this externality may make it difficult or impossible for a market economy to make the right employment decision, and I formalize this idea in the concept of a demand-constrained equilibrium. If this problem can be corrected, the existence of commodity and asset markets implies that a decentralized economy can produce a Pareto efficient allocation.

4.2 Investment and the Keynesian Equilibrium

Economists are used to thinking of general equilibrium in Walrasian terms. Agents take prices and endowments as given and form demands. An equilibrium is a set of prices and an allocation of commodities such that all markets clear, and no individual has an incentive to alter his or her allocation through trade at equilibrium prices.

For the Keynesian model, we will require a different equilibrium concept since, by construction, there are not enough markets to determine equilibrium allocations. This section extends the demand-constrained equilibrium concept of Chapter 2 to the two-period model. I will use this extended concept to introduce the idea that investment determines economic activity, and I will show that there is an interval such that, for any value of investment expenditure in that interval, there exists a demand-constrained equilibrium.

4.2.1 HOW TO CLOSE THE MODEL

Since the Keynesian model is missing an equation, there are many equivalent candidates for an equation with which to close it. Following

The General Theory, this chapter closes the model with the assumption that investors form a set of beliefs about the future. Keynes called this "animal spirits". But this assumption has many representations, all of which are consistent with a self-fulfilling equilibrium. In this chapter, I have chosen to represent the assumption by assuming that the value of capital is determined by the beliefs of investors.

Specifically, let

$$\tilde{I}_1 \equiv p_1 K_2. \tag{4.39}$$

I will refer to $\tilde{I}_1$ as investment, although this is a misnomer since it is in fact the money value of the next period's capital stock. I have chosen this definition because it simplifies the equilibrium concept. By assuming that entrepreneurs have fixed beliefs about the appropriate value of $\tilde{I}_1$, I am able to separate the equation that determines aggregate demand and employment from the equations that determine relative prices. The resulting dichotomy allows me to provide an interpretation of textbook Keynesian models that has a firm microfoundation.

If $\tilde{I}_1$ is large, I will say that investors are optimistic, and if $\tilde{I}_1$ is small, they are pessimistic. I will show that there is value $\bar{I}_1$ such that for any value of

$$\tilde{I}_1 \in \left[0, \bar{I}_1\right], \tag{4.40}$$

there is an equilibrium, characterized by values for prices $\{p_1, p_2, w_1, i\}$, consumption allocations $\{C_1^0, C_1^1, C_2^1, C_2^2\}$, employment L_1, unemployment U_1, productions Y_1 and Y_2, and capital K_2 such that no individual has an incentive to change his or her behavior given the prices and the quantities demanded and supplied for commodities in each period and for borrowing, lending, and capital in the asset markets. In the labor market, employment is determined by matching the equilibrium numbers of searchers on each side of the market.

4.2.2 THE DEFINITION OF EQUILIBRIUM

This section extends the definition of a demand-constrained equilibrium from Chapter 2 to the two-period model with capital. Since this concept is based on ideas from *The General Theory*, I will also refer to it as a Keynesian equilibrium and I will refer to equilibrium values of variables in the model with the superscript K, for Keynes. These values are to be contrasted with the superscript $*$ that denotes the social planning optimum when the planner uses the welfare weights λ_i.

Definition 4.2: (Demand-Constrained Equilibrium): Let K_1 be given as an initial condition and let $\bar{I}_1$ be given by the equation

$$\bar{I}_1 = \frac{(1-b)}{(1-\alpha)}, \tag{4.41}$$

where

$$b = \alpha + g_1(1-\alpha). \tag{4.42}$$

For any $\tilde{I}_1 \in [0, \bar{I}_1]$, a symmetric demand-constrained equilibrium is

   (i) a six-tuple of prices $\{p_1, p_2, w_1, r_1, r_2, i\}$,
  (ii) a production plan $\{Y_1, Y_2, K_2, V_1, L_1, X_1\}$,
 (iii) a consumption allocation $\{C_1^0, C_1^1, C_2^1, C_2^2\}$, and
 (iv) a pair of numbers $\tilde{q}$ and q, with the following properties:

(1) Feasibility:

$$Y_1 \le A K_1^\alpha X_1^{1-\alpha}, \tag{4.43}$$

$$Y_2 \le K_2^\alpha, \tag{4.44}$$

$$C_1^0 + C_1^1 + K_2 - K_1(1-\delta) \le Y_1, \tag{4.45}$$

$$C_2^1 + C_2^2 \le Y_2 + K_2(1-\delta), \tag{4.46}$$

$$L_1 \le V_1^{1/2}, \tag{4.47}$$

$$X_1 + V_1 = L_1, \tag{4.48}$$

$$K_2 = \frac{\tilde{I}_1}{p_1}. \tag{4.49}$$

(2) Consistency with optimal choices by firms:

$$\frac{r_1}{p_1} = \alpha \frac{Y_1}{K_1}, \tag{4.50}$$

$$\frac{w_1}{p_1} = (1-\alpha) \frac{Y_1}{L_1}, \tag{4.51}$$

$$\frac{r_2}{p_2} = \alpha \frac{Y_2}{K_2}, \tag{4.52}$$

$$p_1 = \frac{1}{A} \left(\frac{w_1}{[1-\alpha]\Theta} \right)^{1-\alpha} \left(\frac{r_1}{\alpha} \right)^\alpha. \tag{4.53}$$

(3) Consistency with optimal choices by households:

$$p_1 C_1^0 = \left[(1 - \delta) p_1 + r_1\right] K_1, \qquad (4.54)$$

$$p_1 C_1^1 = g_1 w_1 L_1, \qquad (4.55)$$

$$\frac{p_2 C_2^1}{1 + i} = g_2 w_1 L_1, \qquad (4.56)$$

$$p_2 C_2^2 = p_2 Y_2 - r_2 K_2. \qquad (4.57)$$

(4) Search market equilibrium:

$$\tilde{q} = L_1, \qquad (4.58)$$

$$q = \frac{L_1}{V_1}, \qquad (4.59)$$

$$L_1 = V_1^{1/2}, \qquad (4.60)$$

$$\Theta = \left(1 - \frac{1}{q}\right). \qquad (4.61)$$

In Section 4.3, I will show that a demand-constrained equilibrium exists, and in the Appendix to this chapter, I will show how to compute the prices and allocations associated with this equilibrium.

4.3 Analyzing Equilibria

This section develops aggregate demand and supply equations and shows that the equality of aggregate demand and supply results in an equilibrium employment level L_1^K that is feasible and that satisfies the optimality conditions of households. I call this a demand-constrained equilibrium. An important feature of this Keynesian model is that there is a different demand-constrained equilibrium for every value of $\tilde{I}_1$ in the interval $\left[0, \bar{I}_1\right]$: All of these equilibria have the property that no investor has an incentive to deviate from his or her plan.

4.3.1 AGGREGATE DEMAND AND SUPPLY

As in previous chapters, I choose the money wage w_1 as the numeraire and I define aggregate supply to be the money value of GDP at which employers are indifferent to hiring L_1 workers. The function $\phi(L_1)$ that has this property is found from the first-order condition for labor (4.22) and is given by the expression

$$Z_1 = \frac{1}{1-\alpha} L_1 \equiv \phi(L_1).$$ (4.62)

As in *The General Theory*, I refer to $Z_1 \equiv p_1 Y_1$ as the aggregate supply price of employment, L_1.

Period 1 aggregate demand, D_1, is equal to

$$D_1 = \left[p_1 \left(C_1^0 + C_1^1 \right) \right] + \left[\tilde{I}_1 - (1-\delta) p_1 K_1 \right],$$ (4.63)

where the first term in square brackets is the money value of aggregate consumption and the second is the money value of investment. Using Equations (4.3) and (4.11) leads to the expression

$$D_1 = \left[(1-\delta) p_1 + r_1 \right] K_1 + g_1 w_1 L_1 + \tilde{I}_1 - (1-\delta) p_1 K_1,$$

which, by using the first-order conditions (4.22) and (4.23), can be simplified as follows:

$$D_1 = b Z_1 + \tilde{I}_1,$$ (4.64)

where

$$b = \alpha + g_1 (1-\alpha).$$ (4.65)

This is the point where the definition of investment as $\tilde{I}_1$, the money value of period 2 capital, rather than $p_1 I_1$, the money value of additions to capital, leads to a considerable simplification of the equations that determine equilibrium. If I had chosen $p_1 I_1$ as the object of investors' beliefs, the equation that determines equality of aggregate demand and aggregate supply would have contained the additional term $-(1-\delta) K_1 p_1$. There is no conceptual difficulty in following this alternative definition, but it would break the separation of the equations that determine equilibrium prices from those that determine aggregate demand and supply.

The Keynesian equilibrium occurs when $D_1^K = Z_1^K$. Imposing this condition and solving Equations (4.62) and (4.64) leads to the following expression for the equilibrium value of the aggregate supply price:

$$Z_1^K = \frac{1}{1-b} \tilde{I}_1.$$ (4.66)

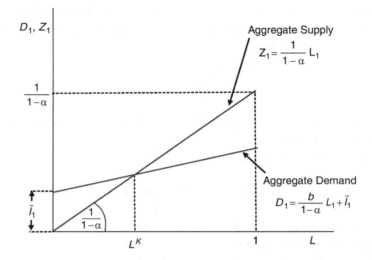

FIGURE 4.1 Aggregate Demand and supply in a Model with Investment

Equilibrium employment, L_1^K, is equal to

$$L_1^K = (1 - \alpha) Z_1^K. \tag{4.67}$$

The Keynesian equilibrium is illustrated in Figure 4.1. Since employment must lie in the interval $[0, 1]$ and aggregate supply is defined by Equation (4.62), it follows that the maximum value of aggregate supply is equal to $1/(1 - \alpha)$. It follows from the linearity of the aggregate demand and supply equations that there exists a Keynesian equilibrium for any value of $\tilde{I}_1 \in [0, \bar{I}]$ where

$$\bar{I} = \frac{(1 - b)}{(1 - \alpha)}. \tag{4.68}$$

The Appendix to this chapter establishes this claim formally by showing how the other variables of the model are determined.

4.3.2 FISCAL POLICY IN A KEYNESIAN MODEL

A Keynesian equilibrium can result in any value of employment in the interval $[0, 1]$, but the social planner will choose $L^* = 1/2$. It follows that, unless investors happen fortuitously to choose the correct value of $\tilde{I}_1$, the Keynesian equilibrium may be one of over-or underemployment. This section describes the Keynesian remedy for this problem by putting fiscal policy into the model.

Since there are three generations, a fiscal policy could conceptually consist of a level of government expenditure and a set of taxes and transfers indexed by the age of the household. I will exclude government expenditure since that raises the issue of public goods, and instead, I will consider policies that consist of an income tax rate τ, levied in period 1, and a transfer payment TR to generation 1. I will show that for any value of $\tilde{I}_1$, there exists a tax transfer policy $\{\tau, TR\}$ that implements the full employment level of employment, L_1^*.[14]

Conceptually, it is possible to tax wage income and capital income at different rates and the generational burden of these taxes will differ. I am concerned with the question, Can fiscal policy maintain full employment? The answer to this question is yes, and further, there are many policies that can implement full employment, each with a different generational burden.

To implement a policy that maintains full employment, let τ_1 be the tax rate on income and let TR_1^0 and TR_1^1 be lump-sum transfers to generations 0 and 1 in period 1. There are no taxes or transfers in period 2 and the tax rate on rental income is the same as the tax rate on wage income. These assumptions imply that aggregate demand is given by the expression

$$D_1 = (1 - \tau_1) \alpha Z_1 + TR_1^0 + g_1 \left[(1 - \tau_1)(1 - \alpha) Z_1 + TR_1^1 \right] + \tilde{I}_1.$$

$$(4.69)$$

The first term on the right side is the consumption from after-tax rental income of the old generation in period 1 and TR_1^0 is the transfer to the initial old. The term in square brackets is after-tax income of the young generation. Their labor income $(1 - \alpha) Z_1$ is taxed at rate τ_1 and they receive a transfer TR_1^1. The parameter g_1 is the marginal propensity to consume for these individuals. It is clear from this expression that there will be many choices of TR_1^0, TR_1^1, and τ_1 that force the equilibrium value, at which D_1 equals Z_1, to occur at the planning optimum Z_1^*; but most of these solutions will cause the government to accumulate debt that will need to be repaid in the second period. Instead, let us confine ourselves to tax transfer policies for which

$$TR_1^0 + TR_1^1 = \tau_1 Z_1. \qquad (4.70)$$

These are balanced budget policies.

Substituting Equation (4.70) into (4.69), replacing $\tau_1 Z_1$ with $TR_1^0 + TR_1^1$, and solving for the Keynesian equilibrium for which $Z_1 = D_1$

leads to the expression

$$Z_1^K = \frac{\tilde{I}_1 + TR_1^0 (1 - \alpha)(1 - g_1) - \alpha(1 - g_1) TR_1^1}{(1 - \alpha)(1 - g_1)},$$ (4.71)

which defines the Keynesian equilibrium generated by any balanced budget fiscal policy. Notice that if the tax rate on wage and rental income is the same, as I have assumed, then a transfer to the old has a positive effect on equilibrium income and a transfer to the young has a negative effect. TR_1^0 enters with a positive and TR_1^1 with a negative sign. It follows that if $Z_1^K < Z_1^*$ (the case of underemployment in the Keynesian equilibrium), the optimal policy is to transfer income to the old, and if $Z_1^K > Z_1^*$ (the case of overemployment), it is to transfer income to the young. The reason is that the young save a fraction g_1 of their income while the old consume all of it, and so a transfer to the old increases aggregate demand while a transfer to the young reduces it.

4.4 Concluding Comments

The main early criticisms of Keynes's work were theoretical, not empirical. It was pointed out that *The General Theory* does not have a satisfactory theory of the labor market. In chapters 2 and 3, I constructed one-period demand-driven models to address these criticisms. Both of these chapters were based on a search-theoretic model of the labor market. Their purpose was to provide a microfoundation to the Keynesian theory of aggregate supply. Recall that the aggregate supply function $\phi(L_1)$ is a relationship between Z_1, the supply price measured in dollars, and L_1, employment. Z_1 is "the expectations of proceeds [i.e. nominal gdp] that will just make it worth the while of the entrepreneurs to give that employment." (Keynes, 1936, p. 24)

Chapter 4 has developed the first, and simplest, of several models that embody Keynes's theory of effective demand. Aggregate demand D_1 is "the proceeds that entrepreneurs expect to receive from the employment of L_1 men" (Keynes, 1936, p. 25) and it can be broken into two components, consumption and investment, each measured in dollars. I have provided a micro-founded model in which consumption expenditure is a linear function of income, and investment expenditure is determined by beliefs of investors about future productivity, so called "animal spirits." A Keynesian equilibrium, formally defined in this chapter as a demand-constrained equilibrium, is a value of employment at which aggregate demand and aggregate supply are equal.

Keynes emphasized that saving and investment are equated not by the interest rate, but by the level of economic activity. This chapter has provided an interpretation of that idea. We are used to teaching macroeconomics in the language of Walrasian general equilibrium theory. In Walrasian theory, prices clear markets and the rate of interest equates saving and investment. By adding a search externality and removing the spot market for labor, I have provided a framework where there are not enough Walrasian prices to equate demands and supplies for all of the quantities. This framework goes beyond *The General Theory* by providing an explicit microfoundation to the Keynesian idea of aggregate supply.

4.5 Appendix

I have shown how aggregate supply and employment are determined in period 1 in a Keynesian equilibrium. It remains to be shown how the prices p_1^K, p_2^K, and $(1 + i^K)$; the consumption allocations C_1^{0K}, C_1^{1K}, C_2^{1K}, and C_2^{2K}; the capital stock K_2^K; and the outputs Y_1^K and Y_2^K are determined in equilibrium.

I turn first to the determination of prices and of the physical value of output, Y_1^K in the Keynesian equilibrium. The equilibrium price in period 1, p_1^K, can be found by solving the equation

$$p_1^K = \frac{Z_1^K}{Y_1^K},$$

(4.72)

where

$$Y_1^K = AK_1^\alpha \left(L_1^K \right)^{1-\alpha} \left(1 - L_1^K \right)^{1-\alpha}$$

(4.73)

is the physical value of output. Using Equation (4.67), this gives the following expression for the money price p_1^K,

$$p_1^K = \frac{1}{A(1-\alpha)} \left(\frac{L_1^K}{K_1^\alpha} \right)^\alpha \frac{1}{\left(1 - L_1^K\right)^{1-\alpha}},$$

(4.74)

as a function of the endowment of capital, K_1, and the value of employment at the Keynesian equilibrium, L_1^K. p_1^K is an increasing monotonic function of L_1^K, reflecting the fact that the real wage falls as investors become more optimistic and the economy moves up the aggregate supply curve. This is the same mechanism that was discussed in chapters 2 and 3.

I now turn to the variables K_2^K and Y_2^K. Given $\tilde{I}_1$ and p_1^K, it follows from the definition of $\tilde{I}_1$ that

$$K_2^K = \frac{\tilde{I}_1}{p_1^K}, \tag{4.75}$$

and hence

$$Y_2 = \left(K_2^K\right)^\alpha. \tag{4.76}$$

Next, consider the determination of real rental rates and consumption allocation to each generation. Generation 0 consumes the amount C_1^{0K}, which is found from the budget equation

$$C_1^{0K} = (1 - \delta) K_1 + \frac{r_1^K}{p_1^K} K_1. \tag{4.77}$$

The real rental rate, r_1/p_1, is found from the first-order condition for rental capital in period 1:

$$\frac{r_1^K}{p_1^K} = \alpha \frac{Y_1^K}{K_1}. \tag{4.78}$$

Equations (4.77) and (4.78) imply that

$$C_1^{0K} = (1 - \delta) K_1 + \alpha Y_1^K.$$

The second period real rental rate, r_2^K / p_2^K, is found from the first-order conditions

$$\frac{r_2^K}{p_2^K} = \alpha \frac{Y_2^K}{K_2^K}, \tag{4.79}$$

and generation 2's consumption is

$$C_2^{2K} = Y_2^K - \frac{r_2^K}{p_2^K} K_2^K = (1 - \alpha) Y_2^K. \tag{4.80}$$

Generation 1's consumption in period 2 is found from market clearing,

$$C_2^{1K} + C_2^{2K} = (1 - \delta) K_2^K + Y_2^K, \tag{4.81}$$

as

$$C_2^{1K} = (1 - \delta) K_2^K + \alpha Y_2^K. \tag{4.82}$$

Finally, we can solve for $p_2^K / (1 + i^K)$, the present value of p_2^K, from Equation (4.12) as

$$\frac{p_2^K C_2^{1K}}{1 + i^K} = g_2 w_1 L_1^K,$$

(4.83)

which can be rearranged to give

$$\frac{p_2^K}{1 + i^K} = \frac{g_2 (1 - \alpha) Z_1^K}{C_2^{1K}}.$$

(4.84)

It is worth pointing out that p_2^K and i^K are not separately defined because money enters the model only as a unit of account.

PART II

USING THE THEORY TO UNDERSTAND DATA

IN THE FIRST PART of this book, I presented three simple models of the aggregate economy designed to illustrate the mechanisms that distinguish a Keynesian from a classical model of the business cycle. All of them were based on the same idea: There may be multiple equilibria in the labor market. In Part II I move beyond the basic framework to develop a series of dynamic models that are rich enough to serve as vehicles to interpret U.S. economic history since 1929.

Any interpretation of the data must first choose which aspects are to be understood. Chapter 5 takes issue with an approach that has become common since Hodrick and Prescott (1997) argued that business cycle facts should be defined to be deviations of observed time series from a flexible trend. Instead, I present an alternative detrending method that uncovers relationships between time series at medium-term frequencies that are missed by data detrended with the Hodrick-Prescott filter. The subsequent chapters interpret the facts defined this way through the lens of the labor market theory developed in Part I. Chapters 6 and 7 present dynamic models to understand the Great Depression and the wartime recovery. Chapter 8 studies the history of the real economy since the Fed-Treasury Accord in 1951.

	A New Way to Understand
CHAPTER 5	Business Cycle Facts

THIS CHAPTER DEVELOPS a way of presenting business cycle facts that differs from most approaches taken in recent work in macroeconomics. Business cycles are recurrent events in which many different time series move together. To present their common features in a way that is apparent to visual inspection, it helps to divide the time series into two components: the trend and the cycle. Almost all recent papers on business cycles have achieved this division by separating aggregate time series into two parts using a method developed by Robert Hodrick and Edward C. Prescott, the Hodrick-Prescott (HP) filter.[15]

The HP filter is a mechanical way of splitting an economic time series into two components. One is a slowly moving "trend"; the other records the deviations from trend. This second component is called the cycle. The Hodrick-Prescott filter contains a "tuning parameter" that can be chosen to make the trend as smooth as desired. At one extreme, it becomes a straight line. At the other extreme, it is the original series. In quarterly data, economists typically set the tuning parameter to 1600, a value that defines a smooth trend that removes decade-long swings in economic activity but attributes movements at frequencies of four to eight years to the cycle.

In this chapter, I will present an alternative detrending method to that of the HP filter. I will present a method suggested by Keynes's discussion of measurement in Chapter 4 of *The General Theory*; the measurement of aggregate variables using "wage units". My purpose for presenting this alternative way of representing data is to illustrate some connections between medium-frequency movements in economic time series that are not apparent in data that have been HP filtered.

5.1 What's Wrong with the HP Filter?

Before the advent of real business cycle theory, in the 1970s, macroeconomists confronted models with data using econometric methods. In the 1960s and early 1970s, the state of the art in macroeconometrics consisted of the estimation of large simultaneous equation models identified by restrictions suggested by Keynesian theory. Usually these restrictions consisted of "exclusion restrictions," the assumption that not all variables appear in all equations. Keynesian models were estimated with systems methods such as maximum likelihood or three-stage least squares, and the estimated models were used as guides by policymakers. A good example is the Wharton model developed by Lawrence Klein at the University of Pennsylvania.

The Keynesian econometric methodology developed by Klein and associates was criticized by Lucas in his 1976 "Critique of Econometric Policy Evaluation" on the grounds that microfounded structural equations should contain expectations of future variables. Since the parameters of these expectations should depend on the parameters of the rules followed by the policy authorities, Lucas argued that the rational expectations assumption would invalidate the practice of using fixed parameter models as policy guides.

The profession responded to the Lucas critique in two different ways. The first, introduced to economists in the (55) book *Rational Expectations and Econometric Practice*, was to develop appropriate econometric methods to estimate parameters in rational expectations environments. The second, explained most clearly in Kydland and Prescott's (1996) article, "The Computational Experiment," was to develop a new methodology, *calibration*, that lowered the standards of what it means for a model to be successful by requiring that a good model should explain only a limited set of empirical moments.

In the introduction to their 1981 book, Lucas and Sargent argued for the development of econometric techniques that would recognize the "cross-equation restrictions" imposed on a model by the rational expectations assumption. These restrictions arise from the fact that the parameters of econometric models are functions of some smaller set of "deep parameters" that represent the true structure. However, when simple RBC models were confronted with data, they often performed poorly.

As a response to this road block in the development of a new paradigm, Kydland and Prescott argued that one could not expect that a science in its infancy would initially outperform established science. In their view, this did not mean that economists should abandon the new approach. They argued instead, that a new paradigm brings its own anomalies and puzzles and that, as real business cycle theory is developed, it will eventually solve these puzzles and supplant its predecessor.

In a related paper, Hodrick and Prescott introduced the Hodrick-Prescott filter that soon became the dominant method for confronting business cycle models with business cycle facts. I will make two separate but related arguments in this chapter. First, I will argue that the correct approach to confronting models with data is the one advocated by Lucas and Sargent and that the new paradigm is now ready to be confronted with a full set of empirical moments. Second, I will argue that the ubiquitous use of the HP filter masks a serious shortcoming of the RBC model and that the use of filtered data to evaluate it overstates the model's conformity with the facts.

The first issue of confronting models with data is beyond the scope of the current work. The second, the issue of presenting limited sets of stylized facts by detrending data, is the main focus of this chapter. I will develop an alternative methodology to the HP filter that corrects a serious shortcoming of the HP approach.

There are advantages to the presentation of HP-filtered data and, properly used, the confrontation of theory with data can be simplified with its careful use. But the HP filter has disadvantages that are often overlooked. Most business cycle models have implications for the comovements of variables at all frequencies. By filtering out the low-frequency movements, one ignores implications of these movements for the relationships between economic variables that could potentially be used to discriminate between theories. Models in which the trend in data is assumed to be generated by a common productivity shock should be filtered by removing a common trend. Instead, the HP filter removes a different nonlinear trend from every series, thereby purging the data of potentially useful information. These low-frequency movements are critical in assessing explanations of unemployment that deny the natural rate hypothesis.[16]

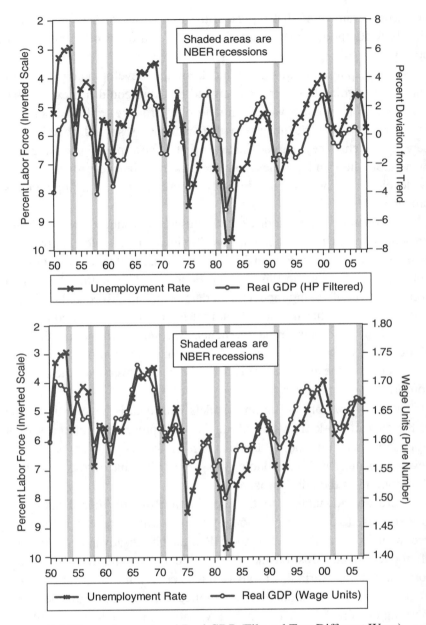

FIGURE 5.1 Unemployment and Real GDP (Filtered Two Different Ways)

The upper and lower panels of Figure 5.1 compare data from 1950 through 2007 that has been detrended with the HP filter with data that has been filtered with my proposed alternative (measuring GDP in wage units). On both panels, the unemployment rate is measured on the left axis on an inverted scale, and real GDP is measured on the right axis.

Notice from the lower panel, where GDP is measured in wage units, that the unemployment rate has low-to medium-frequency movements that move closely with real GDP. Compare this with the upper panel, which plots unemployment against real GDP measured as percentage deviations from the HP trend. GDP measured in wage units moves more closely with unemployment at medium to low frequencies, whereas these movements are filtered out of the GDP series when it is detrended with the HP filter. It is for this reason that I am advocating the use of wage units as a way of measuring real magnitudes.

An example of the kind of movement I have in mind is the slow increase in unemployment that runs from 1969 through 1985, which is mirrored in the lower panel of the figure by a decrease in real GDP. This movement is absent from the GDP series in the upper panel of Figure 5.1, in which real GDP has been detrended with the HP filter.

One would like to be able to ask the question, Did the low-frequency fall in GDP cause the increase in the unemployment rate, or did causation run in the opposite direction? If one adopts a classical approach to the labor market, then the low-frequency movements in unemployment must be explained by movements in the natural rate of unemployment. In a Keynesian model, in contrast, low-frequency movements in the unemployment rate are potentially explained by low-frequency movements in aggregate demand. Since these low frequency movements are not present in the HP-filtered data, it is not possible to address the question of the possible dependence of the "natural rate" on fiscal or monetary policy.

5.2 Measuring Data in Wage Units

What are wage units? The inflationary component of any two nominal series can be removed by taking their ratio. A natural series to use for this purpose is the nominal wage. This series grows for two reasons. It grows because of changes in the value of the monetary unit, but it also grows because the real wage increases as the economy becomes more productive.

In Section 5.4, I will illustrate the behavior of the components of GDP using U.S. annual data from 1950 through 2007. Each series in that section will be described as a per capita nominal series, deflated by the money wage. In all cases, the nominal wage is constructed by dividing compensation to employees from the national

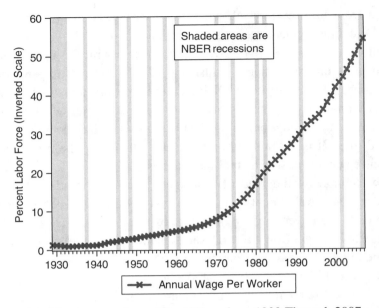

FIGURE 5.2 The Average Annual Real Wage from 1929 Through 2007

income and product accounts by full-and part-time-equivalent employees. This wage series is graphed in Figure 5.2 for the period from
1929 through 2007. These data are measured in units of thousands
of dollars per year. I have chosen to use full-and part-time-equivalent
employees as my measure of employment because it is available con-
tinuously from 1929 through the present day. Because my goal is
to end up with a stationary measure, I also need to remove the
growth in GDP that occurs from increases in the number of working
people.

The number of employed people may fluctuate for two reasons. First,
more or less people may choose to enter the labor force in response
to changes in incentives or changes in tastes. Second, the number of
people employed may fluctuate as members of the labor force enter and
leave paid employment. These two reasons for fluctuating employment
correspond to different economic mechanisms.

Keynesian models account for changes in employment by assuming
a fixed or exogenous labor force and modeling changes in employment
by assuming that the unemployment rate varies with aggregate demand.
Real business cycle models abstract from unemployment and assume
that all variations in employment are caused by variations in labor force
participation. In practice, both margins are important.

The models in this book assume that the labor force is fixed. Just as RBC models ignore the unemployment margin, I ignore the participation margin. For this reason I deflate series in this book by the number of people in the labor force rather than by population. For the reasons discussed later, this measure of GDP per capita moves closely with unemployment.

5.3 Interpreting Wage Units

To see what the use of wage units means in a concrete case, suppose that the data were generated by an economy in which a unique good was produced by competitive firms from capital and labor with a Cobb-Douglas production function using a constant returns-to-scale technology. In this case, the first-order condition for labor would imply

$$bYp = wL, \tag{5.1}$$

where b is the elasticity of labor, Y is the quantity of output produced in physical units, p is the dollar price per unit, L is the number of worker hours used to produce Y, and w is the wage per worker hour. We have data on compensation to employees, wL; the number of full-and part-time-equivalent employees, L; and nominal GDP, pY. In 1929, pY was equal to 103.7 billion, compensation to employees was equal to 51.1 billion, 37.7 million full-or-part-time-equivalent people were employed, and the labor force (call this N) consisted of 47.6 million people. The yearly wage is computed as

$$w = \frac{(wL)}{L} = \frac{51,100,000,000}{37,700,000} = 1,355$$

dollars per year. GDP is computed as

$$Z = \frac{pY}{N} \frac{1}{w} = \frac{103,700,000,000}{47,600,000} \times \frac{1}{1,355}, \tag{5.2}$$

which for 1929 gives a value of GDP per member of the labor force of 1.6 in units of pure number. If we let

$$u = \frac{N - L}{N}$$

be the unemployment rate, then combining this definition with equations (5.1) and (5.2) implies that Z should be equal to the inverse of the elasticity parameter b multiplied by one minus the unemployment rate;

$$Z = \frac{(pY)}{N} \frac{L}{(wL)} = \frac{1}{b} \frac{L}{N} = \frac{1}{b}(1 - u).$$

These calculations show that, if the economy produced a single good, GDP in wage units would be equal to the inverse of the elasticity of labor in production (also equal to labor's share of national income) multiplied by the employment rate. Since there are multiple goods produced in the real economy, this statement oversimplifies the definition, but it is still true that all measurements in wage units have units of pure numbers. To the extent that production technologies are close to Cobb-Douglas, GDP measured in this way is a weighted average of the employment rates in each industry.

5.4 The Components of GDP

This section illustrates some comovements between the components of GDP and the unemployment rate that would be filtered out by the HP filter but that are clear in the data represented in wage units. Figure 5.3 illustrates the comovements of private investment expenditure (top panel) and private consumption (bottom panel) with unemployment. Figure 5.4 shows the comovements of government purchases and net exports with unemployment. In each of the panels of these figures, one of the components of GDP is measured on the right axis in wage units and the unemployment rate is measured on the left axis in percentage points using an inverted scale.

The scale of the left axis, which measures the unemployment rate, is the same in all four panels. The right scale is different for each graph. The investment scale varies from 0.18 to 0.34, consumption varies from 0.92 to 1.24, and the government purchases scale is from 0.2 to 0.52. Net exports vary from plus 0.04 to minus 0.12. These four series together add up to GDP.

The top panel of Figure 5.3 illustrates that investment per member of the labor force moves quite closely with unemployment at high frequency, but there are lower frequency movements that it does not pick up. For example, between 1969 and 1980, unemployment trends up (recall that the axis is inverted) but investment fluctuates around a constant level. In contrast to the stationary fluctuations in investment over this period, consumption and government purchases trend down. These downward

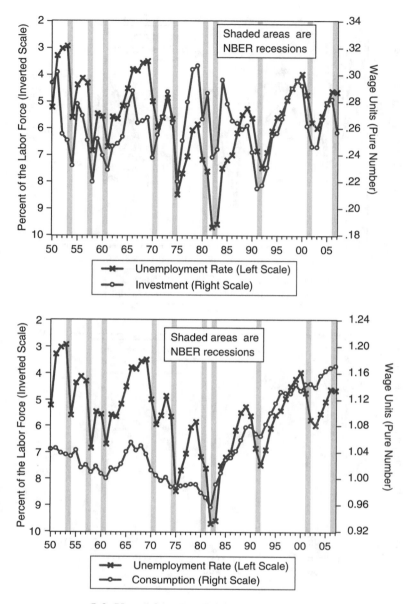

FIGURE 5.3 Unemployment, Investment, and Consumption

trends mirror the increase in the unemployment rate (see the bottom panel of Figure 5.3 and the top panel of Figure 5.4). This period is often referred to as *productivity slowdown* since conventional measures of GDP per person grow at a slower rate in the 1970s.

The model I will develop in this book suggests that the 1970s slowdown in GDP growth was associated with an increase in the

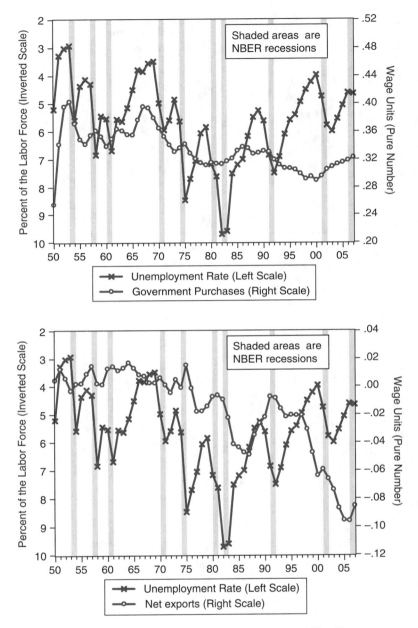

FIGURE 5.4 Unemployment, Government Purchases, and Net Exports

unemployment rate. This increase in unemployment was *caused* by the reduction in government purchases accompanying the end of the Vietnam War. Unemployment depends on aggregate demand and a large component of aggregate demand, is government purchases. In Chapter 7.1, I explain the mechanism that links aggregate demand to

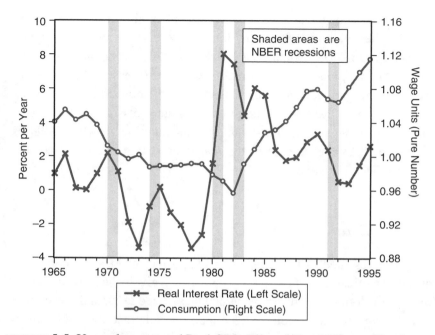

FIGURE 5.5 Unemployment and Real GDP (Filtered Two Different Ways)

employment and I develop a model that can account for the 1970s slowdown.

The graph in the lower right panel of Figure 5.4 represents net exports. This is a relatively small component of U.S. aggregate demand. It displays a clear downward trend since 1980. This downward trend in net exports is associated with growth in the consumption of U.S. households as domestic consumer spending sucked in imports from the rest of the world.

The detrending method that I use in this book reveals a movement in unemployment and the components of GDP at medium frequencies that is not apparent if one detrends data with the Hodrick-Prescott filter. But this correlation is not present in all of the components of GDP. Consumption and government purchases display the same medium-frequency movement as unemployment during the 1970s. This medium term-movement is not present in the investment series.

From 1950 through 1980, unemployment has an upward trend and consumption and government purchases trend down. The movements in unemployment and consumption are reversed after 1980, but government purchases continue to decline. What caused these medium-term-movements?

Figure 5.5 shows that a good candidate to explain the change in consumption behavior in 1980 is the dramatic reversal of monetary policy that occurred in 1980 when Paul Volcker took over as chairman of the Fed. Figure 5.5 plots the ex post real interest rate (measured as the T-bill rate minus the annualized rate of change of the consumer price index on the left axis) against consumption in wage units on the right axis. This figure shows that the turnaround in consumption growth in 1980 is accompanied by an increase in the real interest rate at the time of the Volcker policy initiative.

5.5 Concluding Comments

The data presented in this chapter is suggestive. It does not constitute formal statistical evidence for or against any given theoretical model. But the development of theory is guided by stylized facts, and for the past twenty years, business cycle stylized facts were defined by real business cycle theorists. The RBC agenda is to construct models that can match the volatility and cross-correlations of time series data that has been filtered by removing all but a narrow band of frequencies. By using this limited set of moments, a generation of theorists has been starved of a set of medium-frequency facts. By detrending data in the way described in this chapter, a new set of stylized facts becomes apparent and their explanation provides a new set of puzzles. I attempt to make sense of these puzzles in the following chapters.

CHAPTER 6 | # The Great Depression: Telling the Keynesian Story in a New Way

THIS CHAPTER IS ABOUT the Great Depression. In 1929, the stock market dropped by 11% in one day and, in the subsequent four years, it continued to decline, bottoming out in 1934 at 12% of its 1929 value. Accompanying the stock market decline, unemployment increased from 4% to 24% of the labor force and GDP fell 20% below trend. In this chapter, I use the ideas developed earlier in the book to tell the Keynesian story of this period of world history in a new way.

According to the Keynesian explanation, the stock market crash of 1929 was due to a loss of confidence in the economy that caused a calamitous drop in aggregate demand. This caused an increase in unemployment that was socially inefficient in the sense that unemployed persons could and should have been profitably employed in productive activity. This story was taught to generations of undergraduates as *the* leading explanation of the Great Depression by Keynesian economists of the postwar period. The competition to this explanation was not the RBC model of Kydland and Prescott (1982), but an alternative story of market failure promoted by Milton Friedman (1948). Friedman disputed the impetus to the depression, which for him was the failure of the Fed to maintain sufficient liquidity, but he did not dispute the fact that unemployment during the depression was socially inefficient.

Why do I need to revisit a story that has been accepted by several generations of economists? The theoretical foundations of this story have been discredited because Keynes did not construct a credible microfoundation to the theory of aggregate supply. In this chapter, I use the search model developed earlier in this book to provide such a foundation. In so doing, I will have cause to revisit an important debate that arose in the postwar literature: Does fiscal policy matter?

Before the rational expectations revolution of the 1970s, macroeconomists attempted to extend Keynesian economics to dynamic environments by building microfoundations to each of the components of the Keynesian model. Lucas (1967) and Treadway (1971) estimated models of investment, Milton Friedman (1957) provided a permanent income theory of the theory of consumption function, and Friedman (1956) breathed new life into the Quantity Theory of Money by making the case for a stable demand-for-money function. A central goal of this research was to provide a quantitative explanation of the effects of government policy on employment and prices. This goal ran into theoretical difficulties when economists realized that dynamic optimizing models have no role for fiscal policy since a one-dollar increase in government expenditure is predicted to *crowd out* an equal amount of private consumption expenditure if consumption and investment functions are derived from optimizing behavior by a representative family.

In Section 6.6, I show that crowding out is a logical consequence of the representative agent model, with time-separable preferences, in which government cannot influence the real rate of interest. This fact has important practical consequences for the effectiveness of fiscal policy. If households plan for the future in the way that models of this kind assume, increased government purchases will be offset by reduced private expenditure.

In WWII, there was a massive increase in government purchases of goods and services, and this fiscal expansion was accompanied by a drop in unemployment from 17% in 1939 to 1% in 1944. This recovery is attributed by Keynesian economists to the direct effects of fiscal policy. Since the representative agent model developed in this chapter displays crowding out, it is not a good model of the wartime recovery. Models of this kind have been dubbed "Ricardian" by Robert Barro (1974), who attributes the idea to David Ricardo in the nineteenth century.

To understand the recovery of the economy during WWII, in Chapter 7 I will expand the model by providing an alternative framework in which fiscal policy does matter. This framework assumes that people do not care for their descendents in the way that Ricardian models assume.

There are still important quantitative questions that needs to be answered: Is the world close to being Ricardian, or is the Ricardian approximation a very bad one? If the world is close to Ricardian, then fiscal policy will stimulate employment but at the cost of a very large intergenerational transfer.

6.1 Developing the Model

This section develops the equations of an intertemporal model with a representative agent that has the same supply side that I introduced in Part I. The innovation over earlier models is to add an infinitely lived representative consumer to determine the demand side.

6.1.1 PREFERENCES

I will study a multicommodity intertemporal representative family model in which there is a single capital good in fixed supply. The simplification of nonreproducible capital enables me to draw out a relationship between the value of the stock market (represented by the value of capital) and the level of economic activity.

There is a unit measure of identical representative infinitely lived families. There are n consumption goods and $K_t = 1$ units of capital. Preferences are described by the following logarithmic utility function:

$$J_t = \sum_{s=t}^{\infty} \left[\beta^{s-1} \sum_{i=1}^{n} g_i \log\left(C_{i,s}\right) \right], \qquad (6.1)$$

where

$$\sum_{i=1}^{n} g_i = 1, \qquad (6.2)$$

and the g_i are preference weights. Each family sends a measure 1 of members to look for a job every period. All jobs last for one period and there is 100% labor market turnover. These assumptions are very strong and are made to facilitate the exposition of the model.

The household faces the sequence of budget constraints

$$p_{k,t} K_{t+1} = \left(p_{k,t} + rr_t\right) K_t + w_t L_t - \sum_{i=1}^{n} p_{i,t} C_{i,t}, \quad t = 1, \ldots \infty, \quad (6.3)$$

$$L_t = \tilde{q}_t, \qquad (6.4)$$

$$U_t = 1 - L_t, \qquad (6.5)$$

and the no-Ponzi scheme constraint

$$\lim_{T \to \infty} Q_t^T K_{t+1} \geq 0. \tag{6.6}$$

The notation is defined as follows. L_t is the measure of workers that find a job and U_t is the measure that remain unemployed. w_t is the money wage, $p_{i,t}$ is the money price of good i, $\tilde{q}_t$ is the probability that a searching worker will find a job, $C_{i,t}$ is consumption of good i, K_t is the family's ownership of capital, rr_t is the rental price of capital, and $p_{k,t}$ is the money price of a unit of capital. All of these terms are defined for each date t. All date t prices are in different date t units of account that I refer to as date t money. The variable Q_t^T represents the relative price of date T money in terms of date t money and is given by the expression

$$Q_t^T = \prod_{k=t}^{T-1} \frac{1}{(1+i_k)}, \quad T > t, \tag{6.7}$$

$$Q_t^t = 1. \tag{6.8}$$

I assume riskless borrowing and lending at money rate of interest i_t. A no-arbitrage condition then implies that

$$1 + i_t = \frac{p_{k,t+1} + rr_{t+1}}{p_{k,t}}, \tag{6.9}$$

where i_t is the money rate of interest between dates t and $t+1$. Since all families are identical, there will be no borrowing or lending in equilibrium.

6.1.2 LABOR SUPPLY AND CONSUMPTION

Since the household derives no disutility from work, it will choose to send all of its members into the labor force to look for a job. At the end of each period, all workers are fired and, in the next period, the entire labor force is rehired. I make this assumption to facilitate exposition.

The first-order conditions for the problem are represented by an Euler equation and a set of intertemporal first-order conditions that together imply

$$\frac{1}{C_t} = \frac{\beta}{C_{t+1}} (1 + i_t), \tag{6.10}$$

where consumption expenditure, C_t, is defined as

$$C_t \equiv \sum_{i=1}^{n} p_{i,t} C_{i,t}. \tag{6.11}$$

Equation (6.10) describes how aggregate consumption expenditure, measured in dollars, evolves over time. This equation will be central later in this chapter when I discuss crowding out. For completeness, it is helpful to write down the solution to the household's problem by deriving an equation in which consumption expenditure is described as a function of prices, its time endowment, and the hiring probability. These variables are taken as given in equilibrium. This solution requires first that we define some alternative concepts of wealth.

Let

$$h_t = w_t L_t + \frac{h_{t+1}}{1+i_t} \tag{6.12}$$

be the *human wealth* of the family.[17] By iterating this equation forward and using the no-Ponzi scheme constraint (6.6), human wealth can be written in terms of prices and hiring probabilities:

$$h_t = \sum_{s=t}^{\infty} Q_t^s w_s L_s = \sum_{s=t}^{\infty} Q_t^s w_s \tilde{q}_s. \tag{6.13}$$

The household also has *financial wealth* in the form of claims to capital:

$$\left(p_{k,t} + rr_t \right) K_t.$$

The sum of financial and human wealth is *total wealth*, W_t.

$$W_t = \left(p_{k,t} + rr_t \right) K_t + h_t. \tag{6.14}$$

The solution to the household problem is to spend a fixed fraction of total wealth on consumption goods, and consumption expenditure is given by

$$C_t = (1 - \beta) W_t. \tag{6.15}$$

I will need Equation (6.15) in Chapter 7 when I discuss a more complicated family structure. For the purpose of solving the representative agent model in this chapter, it does not play a central role.

6.1.3 TECHNOLOGY

This section describes the production side of the economy. There is a unit measure of nonreproducible capital that must be allocated across industries in every period. There is also a unit measure of workers, all of whom will be allocated, in equilibrium, to the activity of labor market search. I assume that each industry is described by a Cobb-Douglas production function and that capital is rented in a competitive rental market. Labor is hired in a search market. I assume further that labor in each firm is divided between a recruiting department and a production department as in previous chapters. These assumptions lead to the observation that average and marginal products are equal and are equated to factor prices.

Production is competitive and has the same structure as that described in Chapter 3. Output of the ith commodity is denoted $Y_{i,t}$, and is produced by a Cobb-Douglas function,

$$Y_{i,t} \equiv K_{i,t}^{a_i} X_{i,t}^{b_i}, \tag{6.16}$$

where

$$a_i + b_i = 1 \tag{6.17}$$

and

$$\sum_{i=1}^{n} K_{i,t} = K_t. \tag{6.18}$$

$K_{i,t}$ is the rental demand for capital by firm i and $X_{i,t}$ is the firm's allocation of labor to production. Market clearing in each industry implies that

$$C_{i,t} = Y_{i,t}. \tag{6.19}$$

Firms maximize profits taking $p_{i,t}$, w_t, rr_t, and q_t as given. Each firm solves the problem

$$\max_{\{K_{i,t}, V_{i,t}, X_{i,t}, L_{i,t}\}} p_{i,t} K_{i,t}^{a_i} X_{i,t}^{b_i} - w_t L_{i,t} - rr_t K_{i,t} \tag{6.20}$$

$$L_{i,t} = X_{i,t} + V_{i,t}, \tag{6.21}$$

$$L_{i,t} = q_t V_{i,t}, \tag{6.22}$$

where $L_{i,t}$ is total labor hired by firm i and $V_{i,t}$ is the labor that it allocates to recruiting. Substituting Equations (6.21) and (6.22) into (6.20) and defining

$$\Theta_t = (1 - 1/q_t) \tag{6.23}$$

leads to the reduced form expression for profits:

$$p_{i,t}\Theta_t^{b_i} K_{i,t}^{a_i} L_{i,t}^{b_i} - w_t L_{i,t} - rr_t K_{i,t}, \qquad (6.24)$$

which is maximized when

$$a_i p_{i,t} Y_{i,t} = rr_t K_{i,t} \qquad (6.25)$$

and

$$b_i p_{i,t} Y_{i,t} = w_t L_{i,t}. \qquad (6.26)$$

These expressions are identical to those that hold in an economy with a competitive labor market. This economy differs from the competitive model since the recruiting efficiency parameter Θ_t is endogenously determined by aggregate economic activity but is taken parametrically by the firm; hence, there is an externality in the labor market that is not priced. The following section combines equations (6.25) and (6.26) with consumer first-order conditions to obtain some simple aggregate equilibrium relationships.

6.2 Aggregate Supply

This section derives an aggregate supply equation, similar to that of earlier chapters in the book.

6.2.1 AGGREGATION ACROSS FIRMS

Let the variable Z_t denote nominal GDP. Recall that C_t is the nominal value of aggregate consumption, and since there is no investment or government expenditure, these two variables will be identical as a consequence of accounting identities. My goal here is to find a relationship between Z_t and L_t that I refer to as aggregate supply.

From the solution to the household's problem, it follows that the consumer allocates a fraction g_i of total consumption expenditure to good i; that is,

$$p_{i,t}C_{i,t} = g_i C_t. \qquad (6.27)$$

Since all production of good i is consumed, this also implies that

$$p_{i,t}Y_{i,t} = g_i C_t, \qquad (6.28)$$

and, defining

$$\sum_{i=1}^{n} p_{i,t} Y_{i,t} \equiv Z_t, \tag{6.29}$$

it follows that

$$p_{i,t} Y_{i,t} = g_i Z_t. \tag{6.30}$$

Substituting Equation (6.30) into the first-order condition for the choice of labor in industry i leads to the expression

$$b_i g_i Z_t = w_t L_{i,t}, \tag{6.31}$$

which can be summed over all industries to give the following expression:

$$\chi Z_t = w_t L_t, \tag{6.32}$$

where

$$\chi \equiv \sum_{i=1}^{n} g_i b_i. \tag{6.33}$$

Since money in each period is simply an accounting device, there is a degree of freedom in choosing a price normalization in each period. I will choose the date t numeraire to be labor by setting

$$w_t = 1, \quad t = 1, \ldots \infty. \tag{6.34}$$

This normalization implies that $p_{i,t}$ is the inverse of the real product wage for each commodity, and it allows me to write Equation (6.32) as

$$Z_t = \frac{1}{\chi} L_t, \tag{6.35}$$

an equation that I referred to earlier (in Chapter 3) as the Keynesian aggregate supply curve.

A similar exercise using the first-order condition for rental capital yields the expression

$$\psi Z_t = rr_t K_t, \tag{6.36}$$

where

$$\psi \equiv \sum_{i=1}^{n} g_i a_i. \tag{6.37}$$

In Section 6.3.2, I will use equations (6.35) and (6.36) to describe how the properties of aggregates behave in a demand-constrained equilibrium.

6.2.2 SEARCH AND THE LABOR MARKET

As in Chapter 3, I assume there is an aggregate match technology that results in the following expression for aggregate employment:

$$L_t = V_t^{1/2}, \tag{6.38}$$

where L_t is the measure of workers that find jobs when a measure 1 of workers search and V_t workers are allocated to recruiting in aggregate by all firms. Each firm faces an individual hiring equation,

$$L_{i,t} = q_t V_{i,t}, \tag{6.39}$$

which, when aggregated over all firms, yields the expression

$$L_t = q_t V_t. \tag{6.40}$$

These equations can be rearranged to find an expression relating the measure of workers that can be hired by a single recruiter, q_t, to aggregate employment, L_t:

$$q_t = \frac{1}{L_t}. \tag{6.41}$$

6.2.3 SELECTING AN EQUILIBRIUM WITH LONG-TERM EXPECTATIONS

As in earlier chapters of this book, the absence of markets for the search time of workers and recruiters leads to an equilibrium model with one less equation than unknown. If firms and workers take all wages and prices as given, there is an equilibrium for every value of the sequence of hiring effectiveness parameters $\{\Theta_s\}_{s=t}^{\infty}$. There are many possible ways of resolving this indeterminacy, each of which corresponds to a different possible belief about the future. In *The General Theory*, Keynes argued that the level of economic activity is pinned down by the *state of long-term expectations*. In our model, this concept is represented by a self-fulfilling sequence of values for the capital good, that is, a sequence $\{p_{k,t}\}$.

In an economy with a stock market, $p_{k,t}$ represents the value of equity. In the model of this chapter, there is no underlying uncertainty in the physical environment, but in reality technology, preferences, and endowments as well as political and social variables are themselves changing in unknown ways. In modern macroeconomics, agents are assumed to know the probability distributions of all uncertain future events. In contrast,

Keynes argued that the future is unknowable. As a consequence, the belief of agents in the form of the animal spirits of investors becomes an independent driving force of the business cycle.

In work with Benhabib (1994) and Guo (1994, 1995). I have argued that animal spirits should be modeled by building general equilibrium models in which there is an indeterminate continuum of equilibria, indexed by beliefs and Harrison and Weder (2006) have used this idea to explain the Great Depression. In this work, different equilibria represented nonstationary paths, each of which converges to the same steady state. The model in this chapter is different because I allow beliefs to influence the steady state itself through variations in the state of long-term expectations.

6.3 Equilibrium and the Planner's Problem

This section defines an equilibrium concept and relates it to the social planning solution. As in earlier chapters in this book, one can show that the Keynesian equilibrium mimics the decisions of a social planner by allocating resources across industries in an efficient fashion; but the Keynesian equilibrium may fail to maintain full employment in a well-defined sense. The purpose of this section is to define what this means.

6.3.1 THE SOCIAL PLANNER

Consider the problem

$$
\max_{\{C_{i,s}, X_{i,s}, V_{i,s}, L_{i,s}, L_s, V_s\}} J_t = \sum_{s=t}^{\infty} \left[\beta^{s-t} \sum_{i=1}^{n} g_i \log\left(C_{i,s}\right) \right] \tag{6.42}
$$

such that

$$
C_{i,s} \leq K_{i,s}^{a_i} X_{is}^{b_i} \quad i = 1, \ldots n, \tag{6.43}
$$

$$
X_{i,s} + V_{i,s} = L_{i,s}, \tag{6.44}
$$

$$
\sum_{i=1}^{n} L_{i,s} = L_s, \quad s = t, \ldots \infty. \tag{6.45}
$$

$$
\sum_{i=1}^{n} K_{i,s} = 1, \quad \sum_{i=1}^{n} V_{i,s} = V_s, \quad s = t. \ldots \infty, \tag{6.46}
$$

$$L_s = V_s^{1/2}, \quad s = t, \dots \infty, \tag{6.47}$$

$$L_{i,s} = \frac{V_{i,s}}{V_s} L_s \quad s = t, \dots \infty. \tag{6.48}$$

Equation (6.42) is the objective function of the social planner (identical to that of the representative agent) and equations (6.43) through (6.48) define the constraint set. As in earlier chapters, this problem can be simplified by using the match technology to eliminate $V_{i,s}$, X_{is}, and V_s from the problem. Using Equations (6.43), (6.44), (6.47) and (6.48), one can write the production function for good i as

$$C_{i,s} \le K_{i,s}^{a_i} L_{i,s}^{b_i} (1 - L_s)^{b_i}. \tag{6.49}$$

Using this simplification, the social planning problem can be restated as

$$\max_{\{C_{i,s}, L_{i,s}, L_s\}} J_t = \sum_{s=t}^{\infty} \left[\beta^{s-t} \sum_{i=1}^{n} g_i \log \left(C_{i,s} \right) \right] \tag{6.50}$$

subject to Equation (6.49) for each commodity at each date and the set of labor constraints represented by Equation (6.45).

Proposition 6.1 (SP): The solution to the social planning problem has the following properties. Aggregate employment in each period is given by the expression

$$L_s = \frac{1}{2}, \quad s = t \dots \infty, \tag{6.51}$$

and labor and capital are allocated across industries according to the equations

$$L_{i,s} = \frac{g_i b_i}{\chi} L_s, \quad K_{i,s} = \frac{g_i a_i}{\psi}, \quad s = t, \dots \infty, \tag{6.52}$$

where $\sum_{i=1}^{n} g_i b_i = \chi$ and $\sum_{i=1}^{n} g_i a_i = \psi$.

The proof is in the Appendix to this chapter. As in the earlier models of this book, with a similar labor market structure, there is an optimal unemployment rate of 50%. I will return to this result later when I discuss whether fiscal policy can improve on the equilibrium.

6.3.2 DEMAND-CONSTRAINED (KEYNESIAN) EQUILIBRIUM

In this subsection, I define a *demand-constrained equilibrium,* which I refer to interchangeably as a *Keynesian equilibrium,* for the dynamic economy with multiple commodities. I will proceed to show that a Keynesian equilibrium exists and that it is represented by a set of aggregate equations that determine employment and GDP and a separate set of equations that describe how labor and capital are allocated across industries.

I begin by defining the set of feasible expectations.

Definition 6.1: A (bounded) state of (long-term) expectations is a non-negative sequence $\{p_{k,s}\}_{s=t}^{\infty}$ with a bound B such that

$$p_{k,s} < B$$

for all s.

I define the state of expectations to be a sequence of beliefs about the value of capital in all future periods. In a more general model, there would be a different sequence of beliefs for every type of reproducible capital, and discrepancies between expectations and the interest rate would cause changes in investment expenditures. In this model, I am abstracting from investment spending by assuming that there is a unique nonreproducible capital good. Even in this simple environment, changes in beliefs about the value of capital will have an effect on expenditure since long-term expectations influence wealth, which in turn influences consumption expenditure.

The following definition is of a demand-constrained equilibrium in the infinite horizon economy. Following this definition, I show that aggregate variables in a demand-constrained equilibrium follow a relatively simple equation.

Definition 6.2: (Demand-Constrained Equilibrium): For any state of expectations $\{p_{k,s}\}_{s=t}^{\infty}$, a demand-constrained equilibrium (DCE) is an n-tuple of price sequences $\{p_{i,s}\}_{s=t}^{\infty}$ $i = 1, \ldots n$; a sequence of rental rates $\{rr_s\}_{s=t}^{\infty}$; a set of quantity sequences $\{Y_{i,s}, X_{i,s}, V_{i,s}, L_{i,s}, C_{i,s}, K_{i,s}\}_{s=t}^{\infty}$; and a pair of sequences of numbers $\{\tilde{q}_s, q_s\}_{s=t}^{\infty}$, such that the following equations hold for all $s = t, \ldots \infty$:

(1) Feasibility and market clearing:

$$Y_{i,s} = K_{i,s}^{a_i} X_{i,s}^{b_i},\tag{6.53}$$

$$C_{i,s} = Y_{i,s},\tag{6.54}$$

$$X_{i,s} + V_{i,s} = L_{i,s},\tag{6.55}$$

$$V_s = \sum_{i=1}^n V_{i,s}, \quad L_s = \sum_{i=1}^n L_{i,s}, \quad K_s = \sum_{i=1}^n K_{i,s},\tag{6.56}$$

$$L_s = V_s^{\frac{1}{2}},\tag{6.57}$$

$$K_s = 1.\tag{6.58}$$

(2) Consistency with optimal choices by firms and households:

$$1 = b_{i,s} \frac{p_{i,s} Y_{i,s}}{L_{i,s}}, \quad rr_s = a_{i,s} \frac{p_{i,s} Y_{i,s}}{K_{i,s}},\tag{6.59}$$

$$C_{i,s} = g_i \left(1 - \beta\right) W_s,\tag{6.60}$$

$$W_s = \left(p_{k,s} + rr_s\right) K_s + h_s, \quad h_s = L_s + \frac{h_{s+1}}{1 + i_s},\tag{6.61}$$

$$1 + i_s = \frac{p_{k,s+1} + rr_{s+1}}{p_{k,s}}.\tag{6.62}$$

(3) Search market equilibrium:

$$\tilde{q}_s = L_s,\tag{6.63}$$

$$q_s = \frac{L_s}{V_s}.\tag{6.64}$$

Equations (6.53) through (6.58) define technologies, adding up constraints and market clearing conditions. Equations (6.59) through (6.62) are first-order conditions that define solutions to individual optimizing problems, and equations (6.63) and (6.64) define search market equilibrium.

6.3.3 AN EXISTENCE PROOF

The following proposition, proved in the Appendix, proves existence and establishes the properties of an equilibrium.

Proposition 6.2 (DCE): There exists a unique demand-constrained equilibrium for every state of expectations with bound

$$B \le \frac{\psi \beta}{\chi (1 - \beta)}.$$

In a DCE, for $s = t, \ldots$, aggregate expenditure, aggregate employment, and the rental rate are described by equations (6.65) through (6.67):

$$Z_s = \frac{1}{\psi} \frac{p_{k,s} (1 - \beta)}{\beta}, \tag{6.65}$$

$$L_s = \chi Z_s, \tag{6.66}$$

$$rr_s = \frac{p_{k,s} (1 - \beta)}{\beta}. \tag{6.67}$$

Equations (6.68) and (6.69), which hold for all $i = 1, \ldots n$ and all $s = t, \ldots \infty$, determine the allocation of factors across industries:

$$K_{i,s} = \frac{a_i g_i}{\psi}, \tag{6.68}$$

$$L_{i,s} = b_i g_i Z_s. \tag{6.69}$$

The price in wage units of each commodity is given by the expression

$$p_{i,s} = \left(\frac{\psi Z_s}{a_i} \right)^{a_i} \left(\frac{1}{b_i} \right)^{b_i} \left(\frac{1}{1 - \chi Z_s} \right)^{b_i}, \tag{6.70}$$

and the physical quantity of each good produced is given by the equation

$$Y_{i,s} = \left(\frac{a_i}{\psi} \right)^{a_i} (b_i Z_s)^{b_i} g_i (1 - \chi Z_s)^{b_i}. \tag{6.71}$$

6.3.4 EFFICIENCY OF EQUILIBRIUM

In a Keynesian equilibrium, the value of GDP is proportional to the value of physical capital and is given by the expression

$$Z_t = \lambda p_{k,t}, \tag{6.72}$$

where $\lambda = (1 - \beta)/(\beta \psi)$. Employment, proportional to GDP, is equal to

$$L_t = \chi Z_t. \tag{6.73}$$

It follows that there is a continuum of Keynesian equilibria indexed by $p_{k,t}$. How do they compare with the social planning solution? Since there is a unique solution to the planning problem, it follows that almost all of the Keynesian equilibria are inefficient. There is, however, a special value p_k^*, given by the expression

$$p_k^* = \frac{1}{2\lambda\chi}. \tag{6.74}$$

When the stock market price $p_{k,t}$ is equal to p_k^*, the Keynesian equilibrium implements the social planning optimum and employment, L_t, will equal its planning optimum of $1/2$. If $p_{k,t} < p_{k,t}^*$, there will be inefficiently high unemployment, and if $p_{k,t} > p_{k,t}^*$, unemployment will be too low. In the case of overemployment, nominal GDP is high because prices are high and welfare and physical output could be increased by an increase in the unemployment rate. In either case, if $p_{k,t}$ is too high or too low, the Keynesian equilibrium will be inefficient in the sense that a different belief by investors would result in an unambiguous increase in social welfare.

In a calibrated model that allows for a more realistic rate of labor market turnover, the socially efficient unemployment rate would be considerably less than 50%; perhaps 5% would be a good guess.[18] If unemployment rose to 20% (or higher) as it did in the early 1930s, the additional 15% represents workers that could have been gainfully employed in producing consumption and investment goods. Even if only half of this additional unemployment was due to an inefficiency of the kind modeled in this chapter, the implied welfare loss would be substantial.

6.4 Using the Model to Understand Data

We are now ready to confront the equations of the model with data from the Great Depression and from World War II.

6.4.1 KEYNES AND THE GREAT DEPRESSION—THEORY

According to Keynes, the Great Depression was caused by a failure of aggregate demand. The model developed in this chapter provides a simplified framework for understanding his explanation. In 1929, the stock market fell by 11% in one day. The drop in stock market value

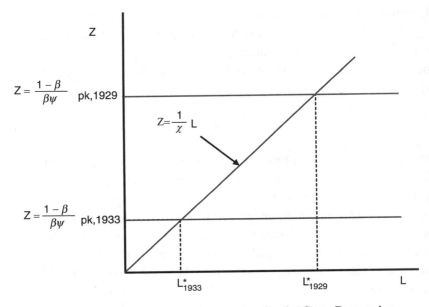

FIGURE 6.1 The Keynesian Explanation for the Great Depression

was followed by a drop in expenditure on new capital goods from 16% of GDP in 1929 to 6% in 1932 and a corresponding dramatic increase in unemployment from 3.2% to 25% of the labor force. The economy did not recover until 1942, when the United States entered World War II.

Figure 6.1 illustrates the Keynesian explanation for these events. In 1929, investors lost confidence in the economy, causing a self-fulfilling drop in stock market prices and a subsequent fall in investment purchases. This in turn triggered a drop in consumption expenditure through a wealth effect.

6.4.2 KEYNES AND THE GREAT DEPRESSION—DATA

In the model of this chapter, p_k is an exogenous driving variable and a fall in p_k causes an increase in unemployment. On the figure, p_k falls from $p_{k,1929}$ to $p_{k,1933}$, and as the economy moves down the aggregate supply curve, employment falls from L^*_{1929} to L^*_{1933}. Is this explanation consistent with the data?

The upper panel of Figure 6.2 plots the value of the Standard and Poor's Stock Market (S&P) index in constant dollars against an investment series and the unemployment rate plotted on an inverted scale. This figure shows that although the model does not explain the investment

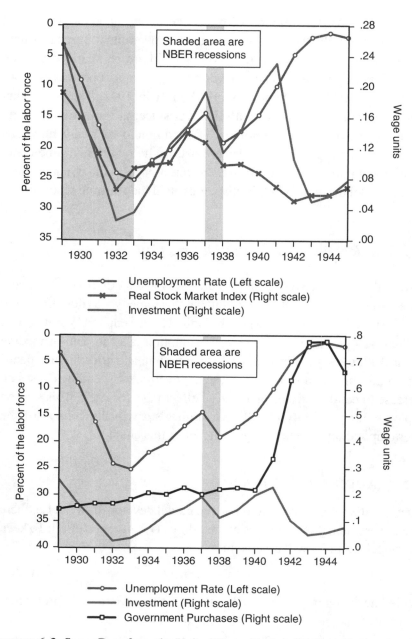

FIGURE 6.2 Some Data from the United States During the Great Depression

data, since capital is fixed, it does capture the increase in unemployment that accompanies the crash. Notice, however, that the recovery in the unemployment rate that occurred in the 1940s is not accompanied by an increase in the value of the S&P index, nor is it accompanied by an increase in private investment expenditure.

The lower panel of Figure 6.2 plots investment, unemployment, and government purchases. The investment and government purchases data on this figure are measured in wage units and are comparable to each other. Notice that although investment falls, government purchases shoot up as the United States enters World War II in 1942. The Keynesian model explains the recovery with this fact since, in the textbook static version of the model, equilibrium GDP and employment are functions of autonomous expenditure, which consists of the sum of investment and government purchases. I now turn to the question, Can the dynamic Keynesian model developed in this chapter explain the wartime recovery?

6.5 The Recovery from the Depression

During the 1930s, government spending was widely discussed as a possible remedy to the Great Depression, but this remedy was not effectively put into practice until 1942, when the United States entered World War II. In the textbook Keynesian model, consumption is a function of income that is itself the sum of investment, consumption, and government spending. In this simple model, an increase in government spending causes an increase in equilibrium income that in effect pays for itself. This section explores the possibility of telling a similar story in the context of the intertemporal representative agent model of this chapter.

6.5.1 ADDING GOVERNMENT

Consider the following variation on the model developed so far. Let there be a government that purchases commodities $G_{i,t}$ in each period. To keep the model simple, I will assume that

$$G_{i,t} = g_i G_t, \tag{6.75}$$

where the weights g_i for $i = 1, \ldots n$ are the same as the preference weights of the consumer. This assumption allows me to abstract from distribution effects associated with changes in the composition of aggregate demand between consumption and government purchases. To pay for its purchases, the government levies an income tax at rate τ_t on labor income, or it may borrow money from households by issuing debt B_t. The assumption that there is no capital tax is not inconsequential since one might wish to use capital taxes or subsidies to influence intertemporal prices. Since tax subsidy schemes of this kind are not the focus of the expansionary fiscal policies that I am interested in, I will abstract from capital taxation in this section.

The government faces the following sequence of constraints:

$$B_{s+1} = B_s (1 + i_{s-1}) + G_s - \tau_s L_s, \quad s = t, \dots \tag{6.76}$$

with the no-Ponzi scheme condition

$$\lim_{T \to \infty} Q_t^T B_T \leq 0. \tag{6.77}$$

Here, $\tau_t L_t$ is the tax revenue from the labor income tax and I have used the normalization $w_s = 1$ to remove w_s from the flow budget constraint. The sequence of constraints (6.76) together with Equation (6.77) is equivalent to the single infinite horizon constraint

$$\sum_{s=t}^{\infty} Q_t^s G_s + B_t (1 + i_{t-1}) \leq \sum_{s=t}^{\infty} Q_t^s \chi \tau_s Z_s, \tag{6.78}$$

where I have replaced L_t by χZ_t from the aggregate supply curve.

6.5.2 CONSUMPTION IN A MODEL WITH GOVERNMENT

How does the introduction of a government that spends, taxes, and issues debt influence the solution to the consumer's problem? Recall that the household solves the problem

$$\max_{\{C_{i,s}\}} J_t = \sum_{s=t}^{\infty} \left[\beta^{s-t} \sum_{i=1}^{n} g_i \log \left(C_{i,s} \right) \right]. \tag{6.79}$$

When we introduce taxes and government debt into the model, the budget constraint faced by the household becomes

$$\sum_{s=t}^{\infty} Q_t^s \left(\sum_{i=1}^{n} p_{i,s} C_{i,s} \right) \leq \sum_{s=t}^{\infty} Q_t^s (1 - \tau_s) L_s + A_t, \tag{6.80}$$

where

$$A_t = p_{k,t} + rr_t + B_t (1 + i_{t-1}) \tag{6.81}$$

represents its initial wealth. Aggregating first-order conditions for this problem leads to the consumption Euler equation

$$\frac{1}{C_t} = \frac{\beta}{C_{t+1}} (1 + i_t), \tag{6.82}$$

and absence of riskless arbitrage implies

$$1 + i_t = \frac{p_{k,t+1} + rr_{t+1}}{p_{k,t}}. \qquad (6.83)$$

It follows from this analysis that the introduction of government purchases does not alter the household's consumption Euler equation. This fact has an important implication for the usefulness of the representative agent model in telling the story of the 1940s recovery.

6.6 Equilibrium with Government

In this section, I define a government expenditure plan and a fiscal policy, and use these definitions to describe the characteristics of an equilibrium in an economy with government. I define a class of fiscal policies that restricts spending by government to have the same distributional pattern as spending by households. Although this restriction is not essential in the sense that one could define an equilibrium without it, the assumption simplifies the characterization of an equilibrium. It would not be surprising if expenditure by government on a particular sector of the economy has distributional consequences by changing relative prices, but that is not what one normally means by the effectiveness of fiscal policy.

6.6.1 SOME DEFINITIONS

A fiscal policy has two components. First, it is a decision by government to purchase a given quantity of goods and services in every period. Second, it is a decision on whether those purchases should be financed by raising taxes or by borrowing.

Definition 6.3 (Expenditure Policy): A (distributionally neutral) expenditure policy is a set of non-negative sequences $\{G_{i,s}\}_{s=t}^{\infty}$ and an initial debt level $B_t (1 + i_{t-1})$ such that

$$G_{i,s} = g_i G_s \qquad (6.84)$$

for all s. An expenditure policy together with a pair of sequences $\{\tau_s, B_s\}_{s=t}^{\infty}$ is called a fiscal policy. If there exists a pair of sequences $\{\tau_s, B_s\}_{s=t}^{\infty}$ such that the budget equation

$$\sum_{s=t}^{\infty} Q_t^s G_s + B_t (1 + i_{t-1}) \leq \sum_{s=t}^{\infty} Q_t^s \chi \tau_s Z_s \qquad (6.85)$$

is satisfied, the expenditure policy $\{G_{i,s}\}_{s=t}^{\infty}$ is said to be feasible for price sequence $\{Q_t^s\}_{s=t}^{\infty}$.

Given this definition, a particular class of stationary policies is of particular interest.

Definition 6.4 (Stationary Fiscal Policy): A feasible (distributionally neutral) fiscal policy is stationary if the sequences $\{G_{i,s}, \tau_s, B_s\}_{s=t}^{\infty}$ do not depend on s.

6.6.2 DEMAND-CONSTRAINED EQUILIBRIUM WITH GOVERNMENT

Given these definitions, I now provide a relatively straightforward extension of Definition 6.2 to show how a Keynesian equilibrium is modified in the presence of government expenditure.

Definition 6.5 (Demand-Constrained Equilibrium with Government): For any state of expectations $\{p_{k,s}\}_{s=t}^{\infty}$ and any distributionally neutral expenditure policy $\{G_{i,s}\}_{s=t}^{\infty}$, a demand-constrained equilibrium with government (DCEG) is an n-tuple of price sequences $\{p_{i,s}\}_{s=t}^{\infty}$ $i = 1, \ldots n$; a sequence of rental rates $\{rr_s\}_{s=t}^{\infty}$ and implied present value prices $\{Q_t^s\}_{s=t}^{\infty}$; a set of quantity sequences $\{Y_{i,s}, X_{i,s}, V_{i,s}, L_{i,s}, C_{i,s}, K_{i,s}\}_{s=t}^{\infty}$; a set of tax and debt sequences $\{\tau_t, B_s\}_{s=\tau}^{\infty}$ such that the policy is feasible for the present value prices $\{Q_t^s\}$; and a pair of sequences of numbers $\{\tilde{q}_s, q_s\}_{s=t}^{\infty}$, such that the following equations hold for all $s = t, \ldots \infty$:

(1) Feasibility and market clearing:

$$Y_{i,s} = K_{i,s}^{a_i} X_{i,s}^{b_i}, \tag{6.86}$$

$$C_{i,s} + G_{i,s} = Y_{i,s}, \tag{6.87}$$

$$X_{i,s} + V_{i,s} = L_{i,s}, \tag{6.88}$$

$$V_s = \sum_{i=1}^{n} V_{i,s}, \quad L_s = \sum_{i=1}^{n} L_{i,s}, \quad K_s = \sum_{i=1}^{n} K_{i,s}, \tag{6.89}$$

$$L_s = V_s^{\frac{1}{2}}, \tag{6.90}$$

$$K_s = 1. \tag{6.91}$$

(2) Consistency with optimal choices by firms and households:

$$1 = b_{i,s} \frac{p_{i,s} Y_{i,s}}{L_{i,s}}, \qquad rr_s = a_{i,s} \frac{p_{i,s} Y_{i,s}}{K_{i,s}}, \qquad (6.92)$$

$$C_{i,s} = g_i \left(1 - \beta\right) W_s, \qquad (6.93)$$

$$h_s = L_s (1 - \tau_s) + \frac{h_{s+1}}{1 + i_s}, \qquad (6.94)$$

$$A_s = \left(p_{k,s} + rr_s\right) K_s + B_s \left(1 + i_{s-1}\right), \qquad (6.95)$$

$$W_s = A_s + h_s, \qquad (6.96)$$

$$1 + i_s = \frac{p_{k,s+1} + rr_{s+1}}{p_{k,s}}. \qquad (6.97)$$

(3) Search market equilibrium:

$$\tilde{q}_s = L_s, \qquad (6.98)$$

$$q_s = \frac{L_s}{V_s}. \qquad (6.99)$$

This definition differs in three ways from Definition 6.2. First, Equation (6.87) is modified to recognize the allocation of resources between household and government sectors. Second, the definition of human wealth in Equation (6.94) is modified to include only the after-tax value of labor income. Third, financial wealth of the household sector, defined in Equation (6.95), includes government debt.

Definition 6.6 (Stationary DCEG): A DCEG is stationary if all variables are independent of calendar time.

I now have enough machinery to define the main idea of this section. I will deal with the case in which households have stationary pessimistic expectations in the sense that p_k is constant and permanently less than p_k^*. Stationarity is a strong assumption but a useful one since it is the case that Keynes believed was characteristic of the Great Depression. In *The General Theory*, he argued that unemployment may be an equilibrium phenomenon in the sense of a stationary state. To capture this feature, I assume that agents' expectations are unchanging and that the economy is in a stationary Keynesian equilibrium with an unemployment rate that is inefficiently high.

6.6.3 AN IMPORTANT RESULT

I would like to be able to model Keynes's prescription of increased government expenditure as a way out of the Great Depression. The following proposition demonstrates that the representative agent environment is not a good vehicle with which to make this case because one dollar of government expenditure is predicted to crowd out an equal amount of private consumption expenditure.

Proposition 6.3 (Crowding Out): Let $\{p_{k,s}\}$ be a bounded stationary state of expectations such that

$$p_{k,s} = p_k < \frac{\psi \beta}{\chi (1 - \beta)}, \quad s = t \ldots \infty.$$

Let $\{G_s\}$ be a stationary sequence of expenditures such that

$$G_s = G \leq \frac{1}{\psi} \frac{p_{k,s} (1 - \beta)}{\beta}, \quad s = t \ldots \infty.$$

There exists a unique stationary demand-constrained equilibrium with government. This equilibrium has the following characteristics. Aggregate expenditure, aggregate employment, and the rental rate are described by equations (6.100) through (6.102):

$$Z_s = Z = \frac{1}{\psi} \frac{p_k (1 - \beta)}{\beta}, \tag{6.100}$$

$$L_s = L = \chi Z, \tag{6.101}$$

$$rr_s = rr = \frac{p_k (1 - \beta)}{\beta}. \tag{6.102}$$

Equations (6.103) and (6.104), which hold for all $i = 1, \ldots n$ and all $s = t, \ldots \infty$, determine the allocation of factors across industries:

$$K_{i,s} = K_i = \frac{a_i g_i}{\psi}, \tag{6.103}$$

$$L_{i,s} = L_i = b_i g_i Z. \tag{6.104}$$

The price in wage units of each commodity is given by the expression

$$p_{i,s} = p_i = \left(\frac{\psi Z}{a_i} \right)^{a_i} \left(\frac{1}{b_i} \right)^{b_i} \left(\frac{1}{1 - \chi Z} \right)^{b_i}, \tag{6.105}$$

and the physical quantity of each good produced is given by the equation

$$Y_{i,s} = Y_i = \left(\frac{a_i}{\psi}\right)^{a_i} (b_i Z)^{b_i} g_i (1 - \chi Z)^{b_i}.$$ (6.106)

Consumption and government purchases of each commodity are allocated as follows:

$$C_{i,s} = \left(\frac{Z - G}{Z}\right) Y_{i,s},$$ (6.107)

$$G_{i,s} = \left(\frac{G}{Z}\right) Y_{i,s}.$$ (6.108)

The proof of this proposition mirrors that of Proposition 6.2 and it hinges on the fact that the household Euler equation is unchanged by the introduction of government. In aggregate, it can be written as

$$\frac{1}{C_s} = \frac{\beta}{C_{s+1}} \left(\frac{p_{k,s+1} + r r_{s+1}}{p_{k,s}}\right),$$ (6.109)

or, using the first-order conditions from production,

$$\frac{1}{C_s} = \frac{\beta}{C_{s+1}} \left(\frac{p_{k,s+1} + \psi Z_s}{p_{k,s}}\right).$$ (6.110)

In a stationary equilibrium, this implies

$$Z_s = \frac{1}{\psi} p_k \left(\frac{1 - \beta}{\beta}\right).$$ (6.111)

Equation (6.111) implies that GDP in a stationary equilibrium is independent of government expenditure and is a function only of the state of expectations. Since

$$Z = C + G,$$ (6.112)

it follows that a one-dollar increase in government expenditure must crowd out one dollar of private consumption expenditure. Since government spending and private spending are allocated in the same proportion across industries, the allocation of each commodity to households and government is in proportion to aggregate spending as in equations (6.107) and (6.108).

6.7 Concluding Comments

What have we learned from this exercise? When economists of the postwar period began to provide microfoundations to Keynesian economics, they turned to the Ramsey model of a representative agent as the simplest formal framework within which to model the evolution of dynamic equilibrium models. The consumption function of undergraduate textbooks was a static function of income. It was soon realized that a forward-looking agent should be concerned not just with current income but also with wealth or in Friedman's terms, "permanent income". The difference between a consumption function that depends on income and a consumption function that depends on wealth has important implications for the effectiveness of fiscal policy.

Keynes argued that fiscal policy can be used to cure unemployment. The textbook Keynesian framework illustrated, in a relatively simple way, why this ought to work. By replacing deficient investment demand by government demand, there would be a multiplied increase in aggregate demand working through a consumption function that depends on income. But if consumption depends on wealth and not on income, then the channel by which extra government purchases should influence aggregate demand is not so clear. If the world is close the Ricardian ideal of Robert Barro, then government debt is not net wealth and a one-dollar increase in government purchases will cause a one-dollar reduction in private consumption. If the world is not exactly Ricardian but close to it, then fiscal policy is a very inefficient way to restore full employment since it requires a massive wealth transfer from one generation to another. The borrowing that benefits the current generation must be repaid by our grandchildren.

The rational expectations revolution of the 1970s threw out the textbook Keynesian apparatus because it did not cope well with the simultaneous appearance of high inflation and high unemployment in the 1970s. But the model could not have been rejected so quickly on empirical grounds if it was not already on weak theoretical foundations. In this book, I have attempted to shore up the theoretical foundations of aggregate supply by providing a sound microfoundation to the idea that there is a continuum of stationary equilibrium unemployment rates indexed by beliefs. This has led me down a road and toward a conclusion that was discussed in the crowding-out debate of the 1970s.[19] Chapter 7 moves forward by breaking away from the representative agent framework and providing a model in which fiscal policy matters.

6.8 Appendix

Proof of Proposition 6.1: Let $\lambda_{i,s}$ be the multiplier on the ith constraint (6.49) at date s, and let μ, be the multiplier on Equation (6.45). The following three first-order conditions follow from the choice of $C_{i,s}$, $L_{i,s}$, and L_s:

$$\frac{\beta^{s-t} g_i}{C_{i,s}} = \lambda_{i,s}, \tag{6.113}$$

$$\frac{\lambda_{i,s} b_i C_{i,s}}{L_{i,s}} = \mu_s, \tag{6.114}$$

$$\sum_{i=1}^{n} \frac{\lambda_{i,s} b_i C_{i,s}}{1 - L_s} = \mu_s. \tag{6.115}$$

Combining Equation (6.113) with (6.114) and summing over i gives

$$\beta^{s-t} \chi = \mu_s L_s. \tag{6.116}$$

Combining Equation (6.113) with (6.115) yields

$$\beta^{s-t} \chi = \mu_s (1 - L_s). \tag{6.117}$$

Together, these equations imply

$$L_s = 1/2. \tag{6.118}$$

To obtain the allocations of labor across industries, combine equations (6.113), (6.114), and (6.116). The allocation of capital follows from a similar analysis using the first-order condition for capital.

Proof of Proposition 6.2: The proof of existence is constructive. Since labor supply is bounded above by 1, and since, in a DCE, $L_s = \chi Z_s$, from Equation (6.35), Z_s is bounded above by χ^{-1}. By aggregating the consumer Euler equations, one obtains Equation (6.10), which can be combined with (6.9) and the market clearing conditions to give

$$\frac{1}{Z_s} = \frac{\beta}{Z_{s+1}} \left(\frac{p_{k,s+1} + rr_{s+1}}{p_{k,s}} \right). \tag{6.119}$$

Using Equations (6.36) and (6.58) and rearranging terms,

$$\frac{1}{Z_s} = \frac{\beta}{Z_{s+1}} \left(\frac{p_{k,s+1}}{p_{k,s}} \right) + \frac{\beta\psi}{p_{k,s}},$$ (6.120)

which can be iterated forward to obtain the expression

$$\frac{1}{Z_s} = \frac{\beta\psi}{p_{k,s}} \left(1 + \beta + \beta^2 \dots \right).$$ (6.121)

Since $\beta \in (0, 1)$ and

$$\lim_{T \to \infty} \frac{\beta^T}{p_{k,s}} p_{k,s+T} \frac{1}{Z_{s+T}} = 0,$$ (6.122)

the infinite sum on the RHS of Equation (6.121) converges to $(1 - \beta)^{-1}$ and rearranging this expression then leads to Equation (6.65). Since Z_s is bounded above by χ^{-1}, it follows that a valid equilibrium requires

$$p_{k,s} \le \frac{\psi\beta}{\chi(1 - \beta)}.$$ (6.123)

Equation (6.66) follows from (6.35), and Equation (6.67) follows from combining (6.65) with (6.119). Equations (6.68), (6.69), and (6.70) follow from rearranging the first-order conditions for the firm and from the following argument. To obtain Equation (6.70), note that the production function for good i can be written, in reduced form, as

$$Y_{i,s} = \Theta_s^{b_i} K_{i,s}^{a_i} L_{i,s}^{b_i},$$ (6.124)

where it follows from Equations (6.23), (6.35), and (6.41) that

$$\Theta_s = (1 - \chi Z_s).$$ (6.125)

Using the fact that the consumer spends a fraction g_i on good i leads to the equation

$$p_{i,s} = \frac{g_i Z_s}{Y_{i,s}}.$$ (6.126)

Combing equations (6.124) and (6.126) and substituting for $K_{i,s}$ and $L_{i,s}$ from (6.68) and (6.69) leads to Equation (6.70). Equation (6.71) is derived similarly.

CHAPTER 7 | # The Wartime Recovery: A Dynamic Model Where Fiscal Policy Matters

T HIS CHAPTER BUILDS a dynamic model in which fiscal policy matters. Fiscal policy works by replacing private demand with government demand. In a representative agent model, private consumption demand is infinitely interest elastic and the real interest rate is pinned down in the steady state by the representative agent's rate of time preference. A one-dollar drop in lump-sum taxes, financed by a one-dollar increase in government debt, has no effect on real economic activity. This property, dubbed Ricardian Equivalence by Robert Barro (1974), has become the benchmark for most recent macroeconomic models.

The overlapping generations model of Samuelson (1958) provides an alternative framework with which to study the effects of fiscal policy. In this model, fiscal policy is effective because the government can influence aggregate demand through tax and transfer policies that shift resources from one generation to another. Realistic versions of the overlapping generations model are difficult to solve analytically since they are described by very high order difference equations. This chapter uses a version of the overlapping generations model that was developed by Olivier Blanchard (1985), based on work by Menahem Yaari (1965). Blanchard showed how to combine the properties of an overlapping generations model with those of the infinite horizon model in a tractable way. Since the Blanchard model assumes that all agents have the same probability of death, independent of how old they are, I will refer to it as the perpetual youth model.

In the perpetual youth model, government debt matters because increased transfers to current generations provide them with real resources, which increases aggregate demand. This, in turn, increases aggregate employment. Debt matters because existing generations do not discount the value of implied future tax liabilities. In Chapter 8, I argue that the postwar behavior of consumption and GDP can be understood in terms of consumption-driven movements in aggregate demand: These movements in consumption are themselves explained by movements in government debt. The current chapter provides an explanation for the wartime recovery based on this same idea.

7.1 The Structure of the Model

I begin by describing the environment, starting with demographics.

7.1.1 HOUSEHOLD STRUCTURE

There are many generations alive at the same time. Generations are indexed by date of birth, and I refer to them interchangeably as households or dynasties. Each household survives into the subsequent period with a fixed probability π. Every period, a measure $(1 - \pi)$ of households dies and a measure $(1 - \pi)$ of new households is created. There are no bequests in this economy, no population growth, and no uncertainty, although these are features that can be added with a little extra algebra.

Each generation has a different consumption pattern, which depends on its date of birth. Because each generation has logarithmic preferences and the same human wealth, it is possible to derive a simple set of equations in aggregate variables that describes the properties of an equilibrium. These equations are similar to those of the representative agent economy, but the representative agent's Euler equation is replaced by an aggregate consumption equation in which income and wealth can affect consumption in the steady state.

As in Chapter 6, there are n consumption goods and $K_t = 1$ units of capital. Preferences of a typical dynasty created at date h are described by the logarithmic utility function

$$J_t^h = \sum_{s=t}^{\infty} \left[(\pi\beta)^{s-t} \sum_{i=1}^{n} g_i \log\left(C_{i,s}^h\right) \right], \quad t \geq h, \qquad (7.1)$$

where

$$\sum_{i=1}^{n} g_i = 1. \tag{7.2}$$

The g_i are preference weights and β is the discount factor. In addition, households discount the future by the factor π to account for the possibility that they may not survive into the subsequent period. The superscript on $C_{i,s}^h$ denotes the birth date of the dynasty, and as in the previous chapter, s and t index calendar time and i indexes commodity.

Each dynasty sends a measure 1 of members to look for a job every period. All jobs last for one period and there is 100% labor market turnover. The dynasty faces the sequence of constraints

$$\pi Q_t^{t+1} A_{t+1}^h = A_t^h + w_t L_t + TR_t - T_t - \sum_{i=1}^{n} p_{i,t} C_{i,t}^h,$$

$$t = h, \ldots \infty, \tag{7.3}$$

$$A_t^t = 0, \tag{7.4}$$

$$L_t = \tilde{q}_t, \tag{7.5}$$

$$U_t = 1 - L_t, \tag{7.6}$$

and the no-Ponzi scheme condition

$$\lim_{T \to \infty} \pi^T Q_t^T A_{t+1}^h \geq 0. \tag{7.7}$$

As in Chapter 6, a unit measure of family members search, L_t is the measure that finds a job, and U_t is the measure that remains unemployed. w_t is the money wage, $p_{i,t}$ is the money price of good i, $\tilde{q}_t$ is the probability that a searching worker will find a job, and $C_{i,t}^h$ is consumption of good i by dynasty h. I have omitted the index h from L_t because the assumptions that families are large and the labor market turns over every period imply that every family will have the same employment level. The terms TR_t and T_t represent lump-sum transfers and taxes that are independent of household.

A_t^h is the family's assets. These are held as pure discount bonds that sell for price Q_t^{t+1}. This represents the price at date t of a promise to pay $1 at date $t + 1$. The household also holds an annuity contract, paid in the form of a further discount of π on the price of the discount bond. In the event that the household dies, the bond reverts to the financial institution that issued it. Although all date t prices are in date t dollars, this is a real model and I choose the normalization $w_t = 1$ for all t. This assumption implies that all prices are denominated in wage units. Hence, $p_{i,t}$ is the inverse of the real product wage for product i.

7.1.2 THE ASSET MARKETS

Household assets, A_t^h, are the liabilities of a competitive financial sector. This sector owns two kinds of assets: the capital stock, K_t, and outstanding claims to government debt, denoted B_t. In aggregate, I assume

$$\sum_h A_t^h = A_t, \tag{7.8}$$

where the sum is over all agents alive at date t. A_t is the total liabilities of the financial service sector. The capital stock, K_t, is valued at price $p_{k,t}$. Government debt, B_t, pays a money rate of interest i_t that is negotiated one period in advance. Hence,

$$A_t = B_t \left(1 + i_{t-1}\right) + \left(p_{k,t} + rr_t\right), \tag{7.9}$$

where rr_t is the rental rate on a unit of capital. K_t is absent from this expression because capital is assumed to be in fixed supply at one unit.

The relationship between the gross return earned by the financial services sector on its assets and the gross return earned by each household on its portfolio is determined by the assumption of a competitive annuities market. The household return includes an annuity payment and hence its return exceeds the market gross return by the factor $1/\pi$.

Each period t, the financial service firms pay the interest rate $(1 + i_{t-1})$ on their liabilities. Since only a fraction π of their liability holders survive, their effective payout is $(1 + i_{t-1}) \pi$. Competition forces the sector to offer the interest rate $(1 + i_{t-1}) / \pi$ to households, which implies that a household may buy a claim that delivers one dollar in period t for the price πQ_{t-1}^t.

The assumptions of no arbitrage and of riskless borrowing and lending at interest factor $1/Q_t^{t+1}$ imply the following two conditions:

$$Q_t^{t+1} \left(1 + i_t\right) = 1, \tag{7.10}$$

$$Q_t^{t+1} \left(\frac{p_{k,t+1} + rr_{t+1}}{p_{k,t}}\right) = 1. \tag{7.11}$$

The first of these equations is the condition that there are no riskless profits by trading in government bonds, and the second is the no-arbitrage condition for trade in capital. The steady-state version of Equation (7.11) implies

$$\frac{1}{Q} = (1+i) = (1 + rr/p_k) > 1. \tag{7.12}$$

Since rr is non-negative, this expression places a lower bound of zero on the rate of interest for steady-state equilibria in which capital is held.[20]

7.1.3 GOVERNMENT CHOICES

As in Chapter 6, the government purchases commodities $G_{i,t}$ in each period and it allocates its expenditure across commodities in the same way as consumers:

$$G_{i,t} = g_i G_t. \tag{7.13}$$

The government faces the sequence of constraints

$$B_{s+1} = B_s (1 + i_{s-1}) + G_s - T_s + TR_s, \quad s = t, \dots \tag{7.14}$$

with the no-Ponzi scheme condition

$$\lim_{T \to \infty} Q_t^T B_T \leq 0. \tag{7.15}$$

As in Chapter 6, I assume no tax on capital and I have used the normalization $w_s = 1$. I have assumed that taxes are lump-sum, as opposed to the proportional labor income tax in Chapter 6. This assumption simplifies the algebra. The sequence of constraints (7.14), together with Equation (7.15), can be combined to impose the following single infinite horizon constraint on government choices:

$$\sum_{s=t}^{\infty} Q_t^s (G_s + TR_s) + B_t \leq \sum_{s=t}^{\infty} Q_t^s T_s. \tag{7.16}$$

7.1.4 THE HOUSEHOLD PROBLEM

Sections 7.1.4 and 7.2.1 draw on the ideas developed in Blanchard's (1985) paper to develop an analog of the consumption Euler equation that holds for aggregate consumption in the economy with births and deaths. First, I restate the problem of each dynasty. This problem is to choose a consumption sequence $\{C_{i,s}^h\}$ to maximize the function

$$\max_{\{C_{i,s}^h\}} J_t^h = \sum_{s=t}^{\infty} \left[(\pi\beta)^{s-t} \sum_{i=1}^{n} g_i \log \left(C_{i,s}^h \right) \right], \tag{7.17}$$

subject to the constraints (7.3) and (7.7). Define human wealth by the expression

$$h_t^h = L_t + TR_t - T_t + \sum_{s=t+1}^{\infty} \pi^{s-t} Q_t^s (L_s + TR_s - T_s) \qquad (7.18)$$

and notice that h_t^h is the same for all families because all agents have the same expected future. Future income is discounted by the survival probability π. Defining C_t^h as

$$C_t^h = \sum_{i=1}^{n} C_{i,t}^h, \qquad (7.19)$$

one can derive the following expression for the value of dynastic consumption expenditure at date t:

$$C_t^h = (1 - \beta\pi) \left[A_t^h + h_t^h \right], \qquad (7.20)$$

which states that the dynasty devotes a constant fraction $(1 - \beta\pi)$ of its wealth to consumption in each period where C_t^h, A_t^h, and h_t^h are all measured in wage units.

7.2 The Aggregate Economy

This section moves from the description of the behavior of households and firms to a set of equations that describes how aggregate variables behave in equilibrium.

7.2.1 THE AGGREGATE CONSUMPTION FUNCTION

Define aggregate consumption, aggregate financial wealth, and aggregate human wealth as

$$C_t = \sum_{h \in \mathcal{A}_t} C_t^h, \quad A_t = \sum_{h \in \mathcal{A}_t} A_t^h, \quad h_t = \sum_{h \in \mathcal{A}_t} h_t^h, \qquad (7.21)$$

where $\mathcal{A}_t$ is the set of agents alive at date t. Household wealth A_t^h and household consumption expenditure C_t^h will be different across dynasties with different histories but, since the preferences lead to a consumption function that is linear in wealth, the consumption functions of individual households can be aggregated. The assumption that makes this work is that

$$h_t^h = h_t, \qquad (7.22)$$

where h_t is independent of superscript h because a dynasty that has existed for a thousand years has the same survival probability as one newly created.

If one thinks of dynasties as people, the literal interpretation would be that a ninety-year-old man has the same life expectancy as a newborn baby. A more reasonable interpretation is that of Philippe Weil (1989), who suggested that we think of these agents as dynasties in which, occasionally, children are unloved and left no bequest.

Equations (7.21) and (7.22), combined with the individual consumption function (7.20), lead to the expression

$$C_t = (1 - \beta\pi) [A_t + h_t].$$
(7.23)

Combining this with the definition of human wealth, Equation (7.18), leads to the following representation of aggregate consumption:

$$C_t = \frac{C_{t+1}}{\tilde{\beta} R_t} + \tilde{\alpha} \left(Z_t + p_{k,t} + B_t (1 + i_{t-1}) + TR_t - T_t\right),$$
(7.24)

where the compound parameters, $\tilde{\alpha}$ and $\tilde{\beta}$, are defined as follows:

$$\tilde{\beta} = \frac{1 - \pi (1 - \beta\pi)}{\pi}, \quad \tilde{\alpha} = \frac{(1 - \beta\pi)(1 - \pi)}{1 - \pi (1 - \beta\pi)},$$
(7.25)

and

$$Z_t = \sum_{i=1}^{n} p_{i,t} Y_{i,t}$$
(7.26)

is the value of GDP measured in dollars and

$$R_t = \frac{1}{Q_t^{t+1}} = (1 + i_t)$$
(7.27)

is the rate of return between periods t and $t + 1$. The derivation of equations (7.23) and (7.24) is contained in the Appendix to this chapter.

In the case where $\pi = 1$, it follows that $\tilde{\alpha} = 0$, $\tilde{\beta} = \beta$, and the model collapses to a representative agent economy. For values of π less than 1, the model behaves very differently from the representative agent model even when π is close to 1. For the case in which $0 < \pi < 1$, aggregate consumption depends not only on expected future consumption but also on income and wealth with a coefficient $\tilde{\alpha}$. Although one might expect $\tilde{\alpha}$ to be small if β and π are close to 1, the model with positive $\tilde{\alpha}$ may still behave very differently from the representative agent model.

7.2.2 AGGREGATE EQUATIONS OF MOTION

This section brings together four equations that, when combined, determine the properties of an equilibrium in this economy. My goal is to derive a graphical apparatus that can be used to analyze fiscal policy in a steady-state equilibrium. The equations are as follows:

$$C_t = \frac{C_{t+1}}{\tilde{\beta} R_t} + \tilde{\alpha} \left(Z_t + p_{k,t} + B_t R_{t-1} + TR_t - T_t \right), \quad (7.28)$$

$$R_{t-1} = \left(\frac{p_{k,t} + \psi Z_t}{p_{k,t-1}} \right), \quad (7.29)$$

$$B_{t+1} = B_t R_{t-1} + G_t + TR_t - T_t, \quad (7.30)$$

$$Z_t = C_t + G_t. \quad (7.31)$$

Equation (7.28) is an aggregate consumption function that describes how current consumption expenditure depends on expected future consumption expenditure, income, and wealth. Since this is a perfect foresight model, at least for aggregate variables, expected future consumption is equal to realized future consumption. Wealth includes the value of the stock market, represented by $p_{k,t}$, and the value of government debt, B_t. Equation (7.29) follows from the no arbitrage assumption in the financial services industry, Equation (7.30) is the government budget constraint, and Equation (7.31) is the GDP accounting identity.

The definition of equilibrium given in Chapter 6 can be modified in a natural way to give a definition of equilibrium for this economy with many agents. The main complication involves recognizing that the allocations of each dynasty will differ according to its date of birth. Once this modification is made, the equations that describe aggregate variables, for any given bounded price sequence, are those represented by equations (7.28) through (7.31). When $\pi = 1$, there is a single representative agent and, in this case, the model collapses to that of the representative agent economy studied in Chapter 6. One might be tempted to think that for π close to 1, the model behaves in essentially the same way. This assumption is not correct as the following analysis shows.

7.3 Using the Model to Understand Data

In this section, I develop a diagram to study steady-state equilibria and use it to analyze a calibrated model of the US during the Great Depression and the wartime recovery.

7.3.1 STEADY-STATE EQUILIBRIA

Imposing the assumption that all variables are time independent leads to the following representation of a steady-state equilibrium:

$$C\left(1 - \frac{1}{\tilde{\beta} R}\right) = \tilde{\alpha}\,(p_k + RB + Z + TR - T), \qquad (7.32)$$

$$Z = \frac{p_k}{\psi}\,(R - 1), \qquad (7.33)$$

$$T - G - TR = B\,(R - 1), \qquad (7.34)$$

$$Z = C + G. \qquad (7.35)$$

A given state of long-term expectations is captured by the self-fulfilling belief that the stock market price will equal p_k. Taking p_k as given and given a feasible fiscal policy $\{B, G\}$, this system describes four equations in the four unknowns R, Z, C, and $T - TR$. The following analysis reduces this system to two equations in R and Z by eliminating $T - TR$ and C using equations (7.34) and (7.35) and replacing their values as functions of Z and R in equations (7.32) and (7.33).

7.3.2 TWO EQUATIONS TO STUDY STEADY-STATE EQUILIBRIA

To facilitate the description and analysis of the steady state of the model, consider the function $g : \left(\frac{1}{\tilde{\beta}}, \infty\right) \to R^+$, defined as follows:

$$g\,(R) = \frac{1}{\left(1 - \frac{1}{R\tilde{\beta}}\right)}. \qquad (7.36)$$

This function is decreasing on $\left(\frac{1}{\tilde{\beta}}, \infty\right)$ and has the property that $g \to 1$ as $R \to \infty$.

Using the definition of g, one can rearrange equations (7.32) through (7.35) to give the following two expressions:

Investment equals saving (IS) curve: $\quad Z = \dfrac{\tilde{\alpha} g\,(R)}{1 - \tilde{\alpha} g\,(R)}\,(p_k + B) + G$

$$\qquad (7.37)$$

and

Interest rate (IR) curve: $\quad Z = \dfrac{p_k\,(R - 1)}{\psi}. \qquad (7.38)$

Equation (7.37) is a steady-state variant of the equation that, following Alvin Hansen and John Hicks, has been referred to in generations of Keynesian textbooks as the IS curve. It differs in two ways from the usual representation of the IS curve. First, the equation recognizes that the government budget constraint must be satisfied and it replaces government expenditure with a function of debt and the interest rate. Second, textbook treatments of this equation assume that the savings rate is constant and the IS curve slopes down because investment expenditure is interest sensitive. In this model, there is no investment and instead, the IS curve slopes down because the Blanchard-Yaari model requires that saving is a function of the interest rate.

7.3.3 THE GREAT DEPRESSION

Equation (7.38) represents combinations of the interest rate and aggregate expenditure that are consistent with a zero profit equilibrium. On Figure 7.1, I have labeled this curve "IR" for interest rate. This curve replaces the vertical aggregate supply curve (GDP independent of R) of textbook classical models. Note also that I have plotted expenditure, Z, on the vertical axis in contrast to the usual textbook convention of plotting R on this axis.

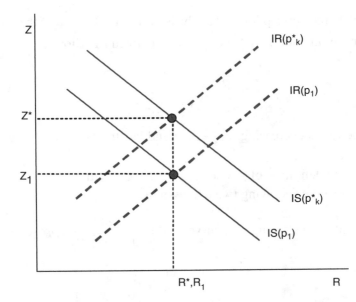

FIGURE 7.1 The Keynesian Equilibrium in 1929 Contrasted with That in 1933

The figure illustrates the effect of a drop in the value of the stock market as predicted by the model. The point $\{Z^*, R^*\}$ represents the model's description of the state of the economy in 1929 before the market crash. This point is chosen in a way such that p_k implements the social planning optimum.[21] The point $\{Z_1, R_1\}$ is the position in 1933, after the crash. The effect of a fall in p_k is to shift the IS curve and the IR curve down. Since the positions of both IR and IS curves depend on p_k, Z is predicted unambiguously to fall, but the effect on R is ambiguous and depends on B. The picture draws the situation for $B = 0$ for which R is predicted to remain unchanged.

7.3.4 THE WARTIME RECOVERY

Figure 7.2 illustrates the predicted effect of a fiscal expansion that raises government debt in the steady state from B_1, its 1933 value, to B_2, its 1942 value. In the data, the debt-to-GDP ratio went from 40% of GDP in 1933 to 120% in 1945. Notice that the expansion in the size of government increases equilibrium GDP but also crowds out some private expenditure since the real interest rate increases and consumption falls.

These pictures and equations are suggestive, but they raise an important empirical question: How well can a calibrated model account for the magnitudes of the changes observed in the data? A first guess at this

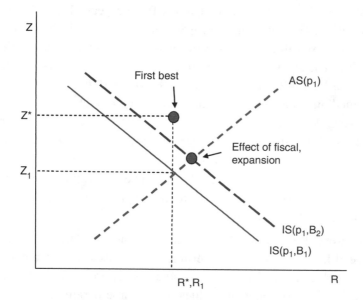

FIGURE 7.2 The Expansionary Effect of Fiscal Policy

question might give a pessimistic answer because of the crowding-out issue raised in Chapter 6. Although calibration of the survival probability is ultimately an empirical question, a model that required very low values of π would not be plausible since it would suggest that the horizon of the average family is short. But if π is close to 1, intuition suggests that crowding out will hold approximately and that wealth effects in consumption in the steady state will be small.

This intuition is incorrect because the magnitude of aggregate wealth effects in consumption depends on the ratio of two factors. In the numerator of this ratio is the compound parameter $\tilde{\alpha}$, which is close to zero if $\tilde{\pi}$ is close to 1. In the denominator is the term

$$\left(1 - \frac{1}{\tilde{\beta} R}\right), \tag{7.39}$$

which is also small if the interest rate is close to $\tilde{\beta}^{-1}$. In calibrated models, these two terms approximately balance each other and there are sizeable wealth effects in the steady state.

7.3.5 A QUANTITATIVE EXPERIMENT

Table 7.1 documents this assertion by studying the effects of a government fiscal expansion in a calibrated model. In it, I compare the values of GDP, government debt, government purchases, and the value of the Standard and Poor's stock market index for the years 1929, 1933, and 1942. In 1929, GDP measured in wage units was 1.6; it fell to 1.18 in 1933 (its lowest value of the decade) and in 1942 had rebounded to its 1929 value. The stock market fell 50% from 1929 to 1933 and had fallen even further by 1942, when it was just 29% of its 1929 value.

I argued in Chapter 6 that the Keynesian model can explain the fall between 1929 and 1933 but that the representative agent version would have difficulty explaining the wartime recovery. By adding the Blanchard-Yaari generational structure, the theoretical possibility arises that the recovery might also be explained since government debt, in that structure, is net wealth. But can the model explain the magnitude of the depression and of the recovery?

To address this question, I simulated the steady state of the model for three different values of government purchases, government debt, and the stock market. The simulated data is reported in the left panel of Table 7.1. I chose plausible values of the three parameters β, π, and χ. β is the discount factor, and I chose an annual discount factor of 0.97.

TABLE 7.1 Fiscal Policy as a Response to a Fall in the Value of the Stock Market

		1929	1933	1942	1929	1933	1942
			Simulation			Data	
Govt.	*Wage units*	0.26	0.47	0.73	0.26	0.47	0.73
Debt	*(% of 1929)*	100	181	281	100	181	281
Govt.	*Wage units*	0.14	0.18	0.63	0.14	0.18	0.63
Expend.	*(% of 1929)*	100	129	450	100	129	450
S&P	*Index number*	11.7	5.8	3.3	0.21	0.10	0.06
Price	*(% of 1929)*	100	50	29	100	50	29
GDP	*Wage units*	0.67	0.40	0.67	1.60	1.18	1.64
	(% of 1929)	100	60	100	100	74	102

$B = 0.97; \pi = 0.98; \chi = 0.66$.

The parameter π represents the survival probability of a dynasty, and here I chose 0.98, which implies that the expected duration of a dynasty is 50 years. The parameter χ is labor's share of GDP, which I set to 0.66.

The results are not highly sensitive to plausible variations in these numbers, although I plan, in future work, to estimate these parameters with more formal methods. Here, I am merely interested in the answer to a back-of-the-envelope calculation to find out if the model has a hope of explaining the data quantitatively.

Next, I assumed that the economy was in a steady-state equilibrium in 1929, 1933, and 1949 and I fed numbers for government debt, government expenditure, and the value of the stock market into the model. I used equations (7.37) and (7.38) to compute the implied value for Z. These numbers are reported in the fourth row of Table 7.1.

The numbers in the left column (which represent the simulation) should be compared with those in the right column (which represent the data). The numbers for government debt and government expenditure are the same in both panels since I fed these numbers directly into the model. The data for the value of the stock market is harder to calibrate since the S&P is an index number. I deflated this number by the money wage to put it into wage units, but the relative importance of stock market wealth and government debt is still not pinned down in the data since it depends on the value of the S&P in dollars at its inception.

I experimented with a number of different values for the initial ratio of debt to real assets. The table reports the solution when the stock market price is equal to 80% of the efficient price in 1929 in a world with no government. This gives the best fit for an experiment in which the depression is explained by a drop in stock market wealth and the recovery is explained an the increase in government debt.

The fourth row of the table shows that the model can reproduce a large drop in GDP, although it overstates the magnitude. Simulated GDP in 1933 is 60% of its 1929 value in the model but 74% in the data. If the stock market price is calibrated to a higher value, the model can reproduce the percentage drop in GDP but it understates the magnitude of the recovery.

Since my computations assume that 1929, 1933, and 1942 are all steady states, it is perhaps not surprising that the numbers cannot come closer than this to the data. Notice also that the model produces GDP of 0.67 in 1929, whereas the true value is 1.6. Since the model excludes investment, this is not surprising.

The main feature that the reader should take away from this table is the fact that a model with long-lived dynasties, each of which has an expected duration of 50 years, is capable of generating substantial wealth effects from government debt and government purchases.

7.4 Concluding Comments

I ended Chapter 6 on a pessimistic note. Although the search model of unemployment can explain the magnitude of the Great Depression, the model developed in that chapter could not account for the wartime recovery. Here, I have amended that model by adding a richer generational structure and I have shown that fiscal policy, of the same magnitude as that observed in WWII, can influence the equilibrium of the economy in a quantitatively significant way. This is perhaps surprising since agents in the model have realistically long horizons and one might think that the model behaves much like the representative agent economy of Chapter 6. In practice, this is not the case for realistic values of the model parameters.

One of the lessons that I learned from this exercise is that although the model can explain how fiscal policy can increase employment, it does not follow that it is the most effective tool to restore full employment. Inspection of Figure 7.2 reveals that if the stock market price remains low, fiscal policy alone cannot restore full optimality. By increasing government debt, the government raises the real interest rate. This moves the economy away from the initial social planning optimum by distorting intertemporal tradeoffs.

In a model with a nontrivial investment decision, government fiscal expansion will crowd out private investment expenditure. Perhaps a policy of directly targeting the price of capital would be a more effective way of restoring optimality? In Chapter 11, I explore this idea further and I suggest that control of an index fund of publicly traded stocks may be a better alternative to monetary and fiscal policy as a way of maintaining full employment.

7.5 Appendix

The budget constraints of the household consist of the sequence of equations

$$\pi Q_t^{t+1} A_{t+1}^h = A_t^h + L_t + TR_t - T_t - \sum_{i=1}^{n} p_{i,t} C_{i,t}^h, \quad t \geq h, \quad (7.40)$$

together with the no-Ponzi scheme condition

$$\lim_{T \to \infty} \pi^T Q_t^T A_{t+1}^h \geq 0. \quad (7.41)$$

The term π occurs on the left of Equation (7.40) because of the existence of a perfect annuities market that permits a household to trade claims to future units of account that are delivered if and only if the agent is alive at that date. A promise to pay one unit of account at date s if and only if the agent is alive will trade for price $Q_t^s \pi^{s-t}$ at date $t < s$. Iterating Equation (7.40) forward and making use of (7.41) allows one to write a single lifetime budget constraint,

$$\sum_{s=t}^{\infty} Q_t^s \pi^{s-t} \sum_{i=1}^{n} p_{i,s} C_{i,s}^h \leq \sum_{s=t}^{\infty} Q_t^s \pi^{s-t} (L_s + TR_s - T_s) + A_t^h, \quad (7.42)$$

or more compactly,

$$\sum_{s=t}^{\infty} Q_t^s \pi^{s-t} C_s^h \leq h_t^h + A_t^h, \quad (7.43)$$

where human wealth of household h, h_t^h, is defined as

$$h_t^h = \sum_{s=t}^{\infty} Q_t^s \pi^{s-t} (L_s + TR_s - T_s), \quad (7.44)$$

and

$$C_s^h = \sum_i p_{i,s} C_{i,s}^h \tag{7.45}$$

is consumption expenditure at date s.

The objective function of the family is

$$J_t^h = \sum_{s=t}^{\infty} \left[(\pi\beta)^{s-t} \sum_{i=1}^{n} g_i \log\left(C_{i,s}^h\right) \right], \quad t \geq h. \tag{7.46}$$

Maximizing Equation (7.46) subject to (7.42) leads to the first-order condition

$$\frac{g_i (\pi\beta)^{s-t}}{C_{i,s}^h} = \lambda Q_t^s \pi^{s-t} p_{i,s}, \tag{7.47}$$

where λ is the Lagrange multiplier on (7.42). Since $\sum_i g_i = 1$, Equation (7.47) can be summed over all goods at each date to give the following expression relating consumption expenditure at date s to its present value price and the multiplier λ:

$$\beta^{s-t} = \lambda Q_t^s C_s^h. \tag{7.48}$$

Substituting Equation (7.48) into (7.43) gives the following solution for λ^{-1}:

$$\lambda^{-1} = (1 - \beta\pi) \left[h_t^h + A_t^h \right]. \tag{7.49}$$

It follows from Equation (7.48) that consumption expenditure at date t is equal to

$$C_t^h = (1 - \beta\pi) \left[h_t^h + A_t^h \right]. \tag{7.50}$$

I now turn to the problem of deriving an aggregate expression for the consumption equation. Recall that human wealth of agent h at dates t and $t + 1$ are related by the recursion

$$h_t^h = L_t + TR_t - T_t + \pi Q_t^{t+1} h_{t+1}^h. \tag{7.51}$$

Let $\mathcal{A}_t$ be the set of agents alive at date t and $\mathcal{A}_{t+1}$ be all agents alive at date $t + 1$. Define aggregate human wealth as

$$h_t = \sum_h h_t^h, \tag{7.52}$$

where the sum is over all agents alive at date t. This gives the expression

$$\sum_{h \in \mathcal{A}_t} h_t^h = \sum_{h \in \mathcal{A}_t} [L_t + TR_t - T_t] + \pi Q_t^{t+1} \sum_{h \in \mathcal{A}_t} h_{t+1}^h \qquad (7.53)$$

where,

$$\sum_{h \in \mathcal{A}_t} [L_t + TR_t - T_t] = [L_t + TR_t - T_t]. \qquad (7.54)$$

Since there is a unit measure of agents at each date, it also follows that,

$$\sum_{h \in \mathcal{A}_t} h_{t+1}^h = \sum_{h \in \mathcal{A}_{t+1}} h_{t+1}^h = h_{t+1}. \qquad (7.55)$$

Combining Equations (7.52), (7.54), and (7.55) with (7.53) gives the equation

$$h_t = L_t + TR_t - T_t + \pi Q_t^{t+1} h_{t+1}, \qquad (7.56)$$

which describes the evolution of aggregate human wealth.

Notice that $\sum_{h \in \mathcal{A}_t} \pi A_{t+1}^h = A_{t+1}$ since the assets of the fraction $(1 - \pi)$ of agents who die are returned to fraction π that survive.

Using this fact, consider the budget constraint, Equation (7.40), which may be aggregated over all agents alive at date t to give the expression

$$A_{t+1} = \frac{1}{Q_t^{t+1}} [A_t + L_t + TR_t - T_t - C_t], \qquad (7.57)$$

where

$$C_t = \sum_{h \in \mathcal{A}_t} \sum_{i=1}^{n} p_{i,t} C_{i,t}^h \qquad (7.58)$$

is aggregate consumption expenditure and A_t is aggregate net financial assets. Aggregating the policy function, Equation (7.50), across agents gives

$$C_t = (1 - \beta \pi) [h_t + A_t]. \qquad (7.59)$$

Rearranging Equation (7.59), substituting it into (7.56), and making use of (7.57) gives the following expression:

$$\frac{C_t}{(1 - \beta \pi)} - A_t = L_t + TR_t - T_t$$

$$+ \pi Q_t^{t+1} \left[\frac{C_{t+1}}{1 - \beta \pi} - \frac{1}{Q_t^{t+1}} (A_t + L_t + TR_t - T_t - C_t) \right],$$

$$\qquad (7.60)$$

which can be rearranged to give

$$C_t \left(\frac{1 - \pi (1 - \beta\pi)}{1 - \beta\pi} \right)$$

$$= (L_t + TR_t - T_t + A_t)(1 - \pi) + \frac{\pi Q_t^{t+1} C_{t+1}}{(1 - \beta\pi)}. \quad (7.61)$$

Define the following constants:

$$\tilde{\beta} = \frac{1 - \pi (1 - \beta\pi)}{\pi}, \quad \tilde{\alpha} = \frac{(1 - \beta\pi)(1 - \pi)}{1 - \pi (1 - \beta\pi)}, \quad (7.62)$$

and notice that

$$A_t = B_t (1 + i_{t-1}) + (p_{k,t} + rr_t).$$

Using the fact that $L_t + rr_t = Z_t$ from the national income accounting identity, we have the following intermediate expression:

$$L_t + A_t = p_{k,t} + B_t R_{t-1} + Z_t. \quad (7.63)$$

Substituting this into Equation (7.61) and making use of (7.62) and of the interest factor

$$R_t \equiv \frac{1}{Q_t^{t+1}} \quad (7.64)$$

yields the result

$$C_t = \frac{C_{t+1}}{R_t \tilde{\beta}} + \tilde{\alpha} \left(Z_t + p_{k,t} + B_t R_{t-1} + TR_t - T_t \right), \quad (7.65)$$

which is the equation we seek.

CHAPTER 8

The U.S. Economy from 1951 to 2000: Employment and GDP

8.1 Introduction

This chapter is about the economic history of the United States in the period from 1951 through 2000. I will ask the question, Can a demand-driven theory account for medium-term movements in unemployment and real GDP per capita? The chapter begins in 1951, when the Accord between the Fed and the Treasury allowed the Fed to conduct active monetary policy. Before that date, the Fed had agreed to a policy of buying Treasury bills at a fixed low-interest rate, a measure that was introduced to facilitate wartime financing. In the period after 1951, the Fed began to control the short-term interest rate in an effort to manage the economy.

At the end of World War II, economists were concerned that there might be a recurrence of the Great Depression but, with the end of wartime price controls, inflation took over as a more immediate concern. A series of recessions in the 1950s was followed by an economic expansion in the 1960s and, during the 1970s, growth slowed down and inflation began to increase. In 1952, the annual rate of wage inflation was 3%, but by 1981 it had climbed to 11%. The increase in inflation was accompanied by a simultaneous increase in the unemployment rate. The coincidence of low growth, high unemployment, and high inflation was dubbed "stagflation" in the popular press.

In 1980, the Fed took aggressive action to end inflation by raising interest rates to unprecedented levels, and the subsequent two decades were a period of high growth, low unemployment, and low inflation. This chapter documents these facts beginning in 1951 and ending in 2000, and it interprets them within the framework of a demand-determined model of economic activity.

8.2 The Impact of the Fed–Treasury Accord

Figure 8.1 illustrates the behavior of a short-term interest rate, wage inflation, and the implied ex post real interest rate for the period from 1929 through 2006. The interest rate is the three-month Treasury bill rate for the period from 1934 to 2006. For the years from 1929 to 1934, it is a six-month commercial paper rate spliced and scaled to equal the T-bill rate in 1934. The rate of wage inflation is constructed from the same annual wage series that was used in chapters 6 and 7 to generate data in

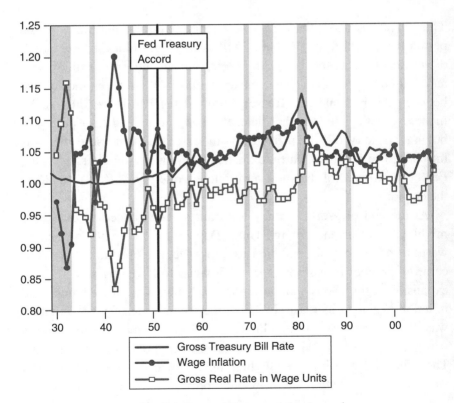

FIGURE 8.1 Interest Rates and the Accord

wage units. The expost real rate is constructed as

$$R_t = (1 + i_{t-1}) \frac{w_{t-1}}{w_t}, \tag{8.1}$$

where i_{t-1} is the annualized T-bill rate between years $t - 1$ and t, and w_t is the money wage in year t constructed as compensation to employees divided by full-and part-time-equivalent employees.

Notice that before 1951, the T-bill rate is smooth and wage inflation is volatile. The period after 1951 is one of less volatile fluctuations in wages but more volatile interest rate movements. Active monetary intervention in the form of countercyclical interest rate movements begins in 1951 with the Accord. For this reason I have chosen to focus on this period in the current chapter. A close inspection of Figure 8.1 reveals that for much of the period from 1951 through 1980, the real interest factor is less than one; this implies that the real interest rate, the real interest factor minus one, is negative. In contrast, the expansion of the 1980s and 1990s is accompanied by positive real rates. The real rate appears to have a trend break in 1980. From 1951 through 1980, it fluctuates around a constant mean that is a little less than one. In 1983, it reaches a peak of a little over 5% and slowly returns to its pre-1980 trend.

8.3 A Preview

Can movements in the components of GDP account for medium-term movements in unemployment? Although "medium-term movements" could be defined more precisely through the use of a band-pass filter to extract a particular frequency, I will not do that here.[22] Instead, I adopt a narrative approach. I ask, How did consumption, wealth, government purchases, and investment behave during historically defined episodes?

The period begins in 1951 with the Fed–Treasury Accord. I will argue that, during the '50s and '60s, aggregate demand was driven predominantly by the requirements of financing the Korean and Vietnam wars. These episodes cause a V-shaped pattern in government purchases that causes aggregate demand to fall as the Korean War ends and to pick up again as the Vietnam War escalates. Figure 8.2 illustrates the movements in government purchases in the period from 1951 through 1980 alongside the movements in GDP. Both series are measured in wage units—GDP is measured on the left axis and government purchases on the right.

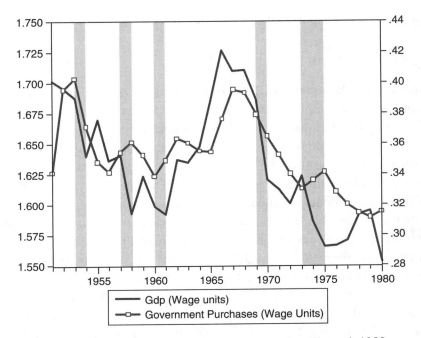

FIGURE 8.2 Government Purchases and GDP from 1951 Through 1980

Although the wartime financing of the 50s and 60s leads to important movements in GDP, it is a sideshow in the post-1951 data, which are dominated by major movements in two components of wealth. I contend that these wealth movements caused consumption-driven movements in aggregate demand.

The first component of wealth is the stock market. I will argue that this variable is governed by what Keynes called the "state of long-term expectations" and it is responsible for a good portion of postwar movements in aggregate consumption. The second component is government debt, which is perceived to be net wealth by households that do not fully discount the value of future tax liabilities. This variable fell steadily from 1951 through 1980 as the government retired the value of wartime debt. This decline was associated with a secular decline in consumption and a consequent fall in aggregate demand.

According to my interpretation of the data, the growth slowdown of the 1970s was caused by the coincidence of a decline in the share of government in the economy and a fall in stock market wealth. Together, these drops in two components of wealth caused households to cut back on spending. The fall in demand was translated to an increase in the

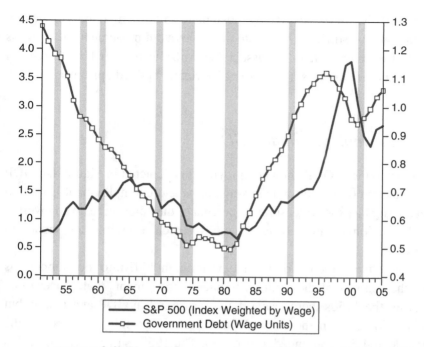

FIGURE 8.3 Wealth Movements from 1951 Through 2005

unemployment rate by the mechanisms discussed in the first part of this book.

The movements in debt and in the value of stock market wealth from 1951 through 2005 are depicted in Figure 8.3. Government debt in wage units is measured on the left axis and the S&P index divided by the money wage is measured on the right axis.

This figure shows that from 1980 through 1996, government debt measured in wage units climbed. The post-1980 increase in debt was associated with a remarkable climb in stock market values. Part of this was associated with high-tech stocks, the so-called dot-com boom of the 1990s. In the theory that I develop here, the increase in the stock market that occurred post-1980 is independent of policy since I model the state of long-term expectations as independent of other economic variables. It seems likely, however, that the stock market began to climb after 1980 because of a change in the direction of monetary policy.

In standard Keynesian theory, investment expenditure is responsible for business cycle movements in aggregate demand that are in turn associated with fluctuations in GDP. In contrast, I will argue that the decline in GDP during the 1970s and the pickup of GDP in the 1980s are associated with consumption-driven movements in aggregate demand that were themselves caused by movements in the components of wealth. Although investment is related to unemployment movements at business cycle frequencies, it is not associated with the principal *medium*-term movements defined as trends over historically defined episodes.

8.4 Unemployment and GDP

The behavior of GDP and unemployment is depicted in Figure 8.4. GDP is measured on the left axis in wage units and unemployment is plotted on the right axis and measured as percent of the labor force on an inverted scale. National Bureau of Economic Research recessions are shaded in gray.

I will divide the period from 1951 through 2007 into four subperiods for the analysis of the medium-frequency movements that concern me. During the 1950s there was a downward trend in GDP and a slow but steady increase in the unemployment rate. Unemployment began the decade at 4.5% and ended at over 7%. The 1960s saw a reversal of this movement and there were seven years of uninterrupted expansion ending with a recession in 1969. From 1970 through 1980, growth slowed down

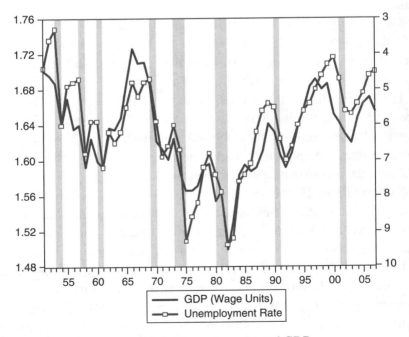

FIGURE 8.4 Unemployment and GDP

and unemployment moved from a low of 5% in the late 1960s to over 9% in 1980. Finally, this medium-term trend was reversed in the 1980s and 1990s with a long expansion punctuated by a single brief recession in 1990 that ended with a second recession in 2001.

In the Keynesian models developed in this book, unemployment is caused by deficient aggregate demand, which is divided into three components: investment, consumption, and government purchases of goods and services. Whereas a fall in investment spending is often blamed by Keynesians for the Great Depression, I will argue in this chapter that consumption and government purchases are more important causes of postwar movements in output and employment. Investment is highly correlated with business cycles at typical business cycle frequencies, but it is not correlated with the medium-term movements in employment that are the focus of this enquiry.

8.5 Investment Is Not a Cause of Medium-Term Movements

Proponents of the Keynesian explanation of the Great Depression often point to the drop in investment expenditure in 1929–1930 as a causal factor for the subsequent fall in GDP and the increase in unemployment. A more plausible interpretation of these events is that investment fell as a consequence of the drop in asset values as the stock market lost 50% of its value between 1929 and 1933.

In the theory I develop in this book, the capital stock is fixed and there is no variable that matches investment in the data. I do not see this as a serious deficiency of the theory since, in my view, the fall in investment expenditure in the early 1930s was an effect and not a cause of a change in the state of expectations. It would not be difficult to construct a version of the theory in which the fall in the value of capital in place would lead to an induced fall in purchases of investment goods.

Additional evidence for the view that investment is not a cause of medium-term fluctuations can be gained by inspecting the movements of the components of GDP in the data since 1951. Consider the upper panel of Figure 8.5, which plots investment, measured on the right scale, and GDP on the left scale. Both series are in wage units. Casual inspection of this figure reveals that local peaks and troughs in the investment and GDP series often occur together, but the broad decade-long swings in

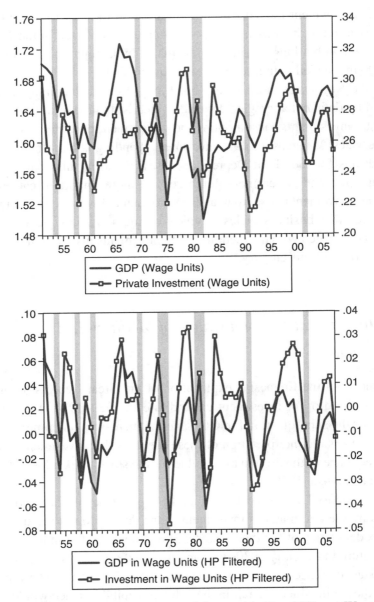

FIGURE 8.5 GDP and Investment Measured in Two Different Ways

GDP are not associated with similar movements in investment. These medium-term GDP swings *are*, however, associated with medium-term movements in the unemployment rate that are often attributed to movements in its natural rate (see Figure 8.4). An example of the kind of medium-term movement I have in mind is the contraction of GDP that begins in 1967 and ends in 1982; this is not associated with any similar discernible trend in investment.

But although investment and GDP are not closely related at medium frequencies, they do move closely together at shorter horizons. The lower panel of Figure 8.5 shows the effect of passing the two series through the Hodrick-Prescott (HP) filter with a smoothing parameter of 100, a value that is commonly used for annual data. The filtered series reveal a much closer correlation of investment and GDP at typical business cycle frequencies. It is these movements that modern business cycle theorists focus upon. The real business cycle explanation for cycles is that they occur as a consequence of technology shocks that cause random fluctuations in aggregate productivity.

In the RBC view, autocorrelated productivity shocks cause movements in investment as businesses expand to take account of future opportunities. In this explanation, investment fluctuations and GDP fluctuations are both caused by the same driving force: productivity shocks.

It is likely that technology shocks are an important source of movements in aggregate economic activity at business cycle frequencies. But medium-term movements in GDP and employment are potentially much more important because they are associated with large movements in the unemployment rate. Existing macroeconomic theory attributes these medium-term movements to changes in the natural rate of unemployment. I argue instead that they are caused by changes in aggregate demand.

As an example, consider the medium-frequency movement in GDP that began with the 1967 peak and ended with the 1982 trough. This was a movement of 2 wage units from 1.72 to 1.52. Although the lower panel of Figure 8.5 reveals that this movement was associated with a spike in HP-filtered investment in 1967 and a trough in 1982, the upper panel of the figure reveals that that investment was acyclic over the decade. Because a productivity shock should cause GDP and investment to move together, the medium-term downward trend in GDP from 1967 through 1982 cannot have been caused by a productivity shock.

8.6 Other Possible Causes of Medium-Term Fluctuations

In addition to investment spending, aggregate demand movements may be due to changes in consumption that are themselves driven by

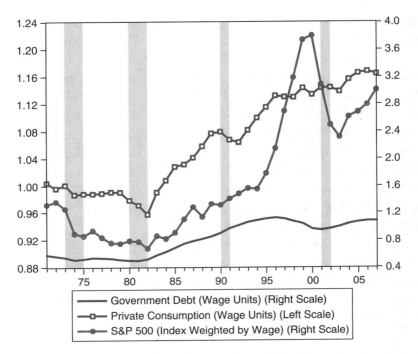

FIGURE 8.6 Consumption and Wealth

movements in wealth and income. They may also be caused by movements in government purchases. This section studies each of these possibilities in the context of the history of changes in GDP since 1951.

Figure 8.6 depicts consumption, stock market wealth, and government debt from 1971 through 2006. Government debt and the Standard and Poor's index are measured on the right axis and the value of consumption is measured on the left axis. Consistently measuring stock market wealth is potentially a problem because the device of measuring all variables in wage units cannot be directly applied to the Standard and Poor's (henceforth the S&P) since the S&P is an index number and is not measured in dollars.

To handle this issue, I divided the S&P by the money wage to give a series with units of inverse dollars. Movements in government debt are directly comparable with movements in stock market wealth, but the levels of the two series depends on an arbitrary normalization.[23]

Let's consider how the model developed in Chapter 7 attributes importance to the components of aggregate demand as explanatory factors in causing movements in GDP. This model has a steady-state consumption function with the following functional form:

$$C = \tilde{\alpha} g(R)(p_k + B + Z), \qquad (8.2)$$

where Equation (8.2) combines (7.32) and (7.33) and

$$g(R) \equiv \frac{1}{1 - \frac{1}{\tilde{\beta}R}}. \qquad (8.3)$$

Using the income accounting identity, one can derive the following equation that describes steady-state GDP:

$$Z = H(R)(p_k + BR) + G, \qquad (8.4)$$

where

$$H(R) \equiv \frac{\tilde{\alpha} g(R)}{1 - \tilde{\alpha} g(R)}. \qquad (8.5)$$

Recall that Z is GDP, B is government debt, p_k is the value of the stock market, and R is the gross rate of interest. The following explanation is based on the two steady-state equations, (8.2) and (8.4), and although the relative importance of the different determinants of consumption and income will depend on the timing of events and on equilibrium dynamics, the steady-state equations will give a rough picture of the plausibility of a demand-driven explanation.

How well does a theory based on equations (8.2) and (8.4) explain the facts? Figure 8.7 plots GDP on the left axis and government purchases on the right from 1951 through 2007. Both series are measured in wage units. From 1951 through 1971, demand movements are dominated by changes in government purchases caused by the end of the Korean War and the beginning and end of the Vietnam War. Notice, from Figure 8.7, how closely these GDP and government purchases move together over this period. These co-movements are accounted for, in theory, by the appearance of the term G in Equation (8.4). After 1971, GDP trends downward until 1980, at which point it reverses direction and begins a sharp upward trend. Figure 8.6 shows that consumption and wealth have the same pattern. These movements are accounted for in the theory by the appearance of the wealth terms p_k and B in Equation 8.4.

The pictures I have presented suggest that the Keynesian explanation can account qualitatively for the data since 1951. However, without a more formal econometric analysis, it is difficult to assess the quantitative success of my explanation. One would like to know if the magnitude of the wealth elasticity of consumption is similar in the Great Depression

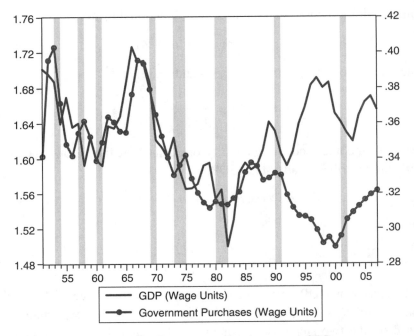

FIGURE 8.7 Government Purchases and GDP

and the postwar years. Is stock market wealth comparable in magnitude to government debt? What is the importance of endogenous consumption dynamics in helping to explain the facts? Can the addition of housing wealth add explanatory power, as the 2008 crisis in the market for mortgage-backed securities suggests it might? These are all important questions that I will address in future empirical work.

8.7 Concluding Comments

Most recent studies of the postwar business cycle *define* the cycle as a series of comovements between HP-filtered time series. The real business cycle model, which explains the cycle as a set of optimal responses to an autocorrelated series of productivity shocks, is relatively successful at capturing these comovements, and I have no doubt that this explanation is an important component of any successful theory of business cycles. My objection to the real business cycle approach is that the filtered data cannot explain movements at medium-term frequencies, which must instead be attributed to movements in "the natural rate of unemployment." In this chapter, I have studied the plausibility of an alternative demand-driven theory by examining the comovements of the components of aggregate demand with movements in unemployment and GDP.

To summarize the argument: In my theory, aggregate demand has three main determinants: government purchases, government debt, and the value of the stock market. In the period from 1951 to 1970, the major movements in government purchases were driven by the requirements of wartime financing. Those movements were responsible for a slowdown in the 1950s and a subsequent expansion in the 1960s. Superimposed on the movements in government purchases, there was a decline in government debt from 1951 through 1979 that was subsequently reversed and followed by a period of increasing debt. As government debt increased, it fueled a consumption-led boom in economic activity as current generations borrowed from future generations. A contributing factor to the boom of the 1980s and 1990s was a buildup of confidence, reflected in a huge stock market bubble. The bursting of this bubble led to the Great Recession of 2008.

PART III

THE THEORY OF PRICES

THE MODELS I HAVE used so far have ignored money and uncertainty. In Part III, I introduce both of these elements. Chapter 9 brings money into a stochastic version of the model from Chapter 6. Chapter 10 continues the narrative account from Part II by describing the monetary features of the economy since 1951. These chapters provide a framework for studying monetary policy in a dynamic stochastic environment, but the analysis of the model is left for future work. Chapter 11 describes a new institution, as an alternative to fiscal policy, that provides an alternative way of regulating excessive swings in the market economy.

CHAPTER 9

Money and Uncertainty

I N PART II, I EXPLAINED the economic history of the US since 1929 using a model with no money that did not allow for uncertainty. In this chapter, I bring in both money and uncertainty and I develop a model that can be used to understand how unemployment and inflation can coexist.

To include money, I assume that it is a productive factor like labor and capital. To include uncertainty, I assume that there is a finite set of states in each period and agents are able to trade a complete set of Arrow securities.[24]

9.1 The Structure of the Model

In Section 9.1, I introduce money by assuming that it acts as a productive factor. This shortcut, first used by Patinkin (1956), has a distinguished history in economics. It is meant to represent the benefit that accrues to the firm from using cash in transactions.

9.1.1 MONEY AND PRODUCTION

I will assume the same production sector as in Chapter 6 with the exception that each good is produced with money as well as with capital and labor. As in that chapter, labor is hired in a competitive search market and firms take the wage w_t, the prices $p_{i,t}$, for each good i, and the hiring effectiveness of a recruiter q_t as given. There are n commodities. Recall that in this structure each firm faces the production function

$$Y_{i,t} = K_{i,t}^{a_i} X_{i,t}^{b_i} m_{i,t}^{h_i}, \tag{9.1}$$

and the labor market constraints

$$L_{i,t} = X_{i,t} + V_{i,t}, \tag{9.2}$$

$$L_{i,t} = q_t V_{i,t}, \tag{9.3}$$

where

$$a_i + b_i + h_i = 1. \tag{9.4}$$

In Equation (9.1), I have modified the model of Chapter 6 by adding money,

$$m_{i,t} = \frac{M_{i,t}}{p_{i,t}}. \tag{9.5}$$

$m_{i,t}$ represents the value of money balances measured in units of the firm's output price at date t. Money is held by the financial services sector and "rented" to firms at rate i_{t-1}. Since the use of money at date t is negotiated at date $t - 1$, the relative price of date t money is the date $t - 1$ interest rate, i_{t-1}. A slight modification to the argument from Chapter 6 gives the first-order conditions

$$b_i \, p_{i,t} Y_{i,t} = w_t L_t, \tag{9.6}$$

$$a_i \, p_{i,t} Y_{i,t} = rr_t K_{i,t}, \tag{9.7}$$

$$h_i \, p_{i,t} Y_{i,t} = i_{t-1} M_{i,t}, \tag{9.8}$$

and aggregating across industries yields the aggregate supply curve,

$$\chi Z_t = w_t L_t; \tag{9.9}$$

the definition of the rental rate,

$$\psi Z_t = rr_t; \tag{9.10}$$

and a new expression, which represents a demand function for money,

$$h Z_t = i_{t-1} M_t. \tag{9.11}$$

The parameters χ and ψ are defined as in earlier chapters and h is defined in Equation (9.12):

$$h = \sum g_i h_i. \tag{9.12}$$

I will be studying policies in which the Fed controls the interest rate through open market operations. In this framework, the demand-for-money function, Equation (9.11), determines the money supply.

9.1.2 ADDING UNCERTAINTY

To introduce uncertainty I assume that in each period one of N uncertain states may occur. The set of one-period states is $\mathbf{S} = \{S_1, \ldots, S_N\}$, and a realization of a state is called an event. A set of t events that occurs sequentially is called a t-period history. The set of t-period histories, $\mathbf{S}^t$, is defined recursively as follows:

$$\mathbf{S}^1 = \mathbf{S}, \tag{9.13}$$

$$\mathbf{S}^t = \mathbf{S}^{t-1} \times \mathbf{S}, t = 2, \ldots \tag{9.14}$$

Because I want to highlight the effects of self-fulfilling beliefs, I assume that all uncertainty is nonfundamental in the sense that it affects beliefs but it does not affect preferences, technologies, or endowments. These are "sunspot shocks" in the sense of Cass and Shell (1983). This assumption can easily be modified to allow for fundamental shocks.

Agents are permitted to trade securities contingent on the states of nature, and I assume agents trade a complete set of Arrow securities to insure against uncertainty. $Q_t^s(S_j^s)$ denotes the price of a security that pays one unit of money if and only if the history $S_j^s \in \mathbf{S}^s$ occurs at date s. Assets held by the representative household are given by the following identity:

$$A_t = (B_t + M_t)(1 + i_{t-1}) + (p_{k,t} + rr_t) K_t, \tag{9.15}$$

where I assume

$$K_t = 1 \tag{9.16}$$

as in previous chapters.

Equation (9.15) decomposes household assets into three components: government debt, money, and private capital. Each of these assets pays a return. One dollar of government debt or one dollar of money, issued at date $t - 1$, pays $1 + i_{t-1}$ units of money in date t in all states. In the case of government debt, the interest is paid by government. In the case of money, it is paid by firms who negotiate loans in period $t - 1$ for the use of money in period t. Private capital pays the money rental rate rr_t.

9.1.3 HOUSEHOLDS

The representative household maximizes expected utility and has logarithmic preferences. Households trade financial assets in the form of Arrow securities A_t. Agents are assumed to maximize the function

$$J_t = E_t \sum_{s=t}^{\infty} \left[\beta^{s-t} \sum_{i=1}^{n} g_i \log \left(C_{i,s} \right) \right], \tag{9.17}$$

subject to the sequence of constraints

$$w_s L_s + TR_s - T_s + A_s$$
$$= \sum_{j=1}^{N} Q_s^{s+1} \left(S_j \right) A_{s+1} \left(S_j \right) + \sum_{i=1}^{n} p_{i,s} C_{i,s}, \quad s = t, \dots \tag{9.18}$$

The expectations operator in Equation (9.17) is over realizations of all future state-contingent histories.

The labor market is identical to that described in earlier chapters. Each household sends a measure 1 of workers to look for jobs in each period. $\tilde{q}_s$ of these workers find jobs and earn money wage w_s. $p_{i,s}$ is the price and $C_{i,s}$ is the quantity of goods i consumed at date s. TR_s and T_s are lump-sum transfers and taxes. The no-Ponzi conditions must also hold in each history:

$$\lim_{T \to \infty} Q_t^T \left(S_j^T \right) A_{T+1} \left(S_j^T \right) \geq 0, \quad \text{for all } S_j^T \in \mathbf{S}^T. \tag{9.19}$$

Together, Equations (9.18) and (9.19) imply the existence of a single budget constraint,

$$\sum_{s=t}^{\infty} \sum_{j=1}^{N_t^s} Q_t^s \left(\sum_{i=1}^{n} p_{i,s} \left(S_j^s \right) C_{i,s} \left(S_j^s \right) \right) \leq h_t + A_t, \tag{9.20}$$

where human wealth is defined recursively by the expression

$$h_t = w_t L_t + TR_t - T_t + \sum_{j=1}^{N} \left[Q_t^{t+1} \left(S_j^{t+1} \right) h_{t+1} \left(S_j^{t+1} \right) \right], \tag{9.21}$$

plus the assumption that the net present value of after-tax labor income is finite, which places a limit on the set of feasible pricing kernels to those for which the state-dependent prices do not grow "too fast". One may derive the following closed form solution for the expenditure of the household on good i:

$$p_{i,t}C_{i,t} = (1 - \beta) g_i [h_t + A_t].\qquad(9.22)$$

Summing Equation (9.22) over all commodities yields

$$C_t = (1 - \beta) [h_t + A_t],\qquad(9.23)$$

where

$$C_t = \sum_{i=1}^{n} p_{i,t} (S_j) C_{i,t}\qquad(9.24)$$

is the money value of consumption expenditure by the household.

9.1.4 GOVERNMENT

As in the previous chapters of this book, I model government mechanically. Here, that implies that government chooses sequences $\{TR_t, T_t, M_{t+1} + B_{t+1}\}$ to satisfy the constraints

$$B_{t+1} + M_{t+1} = B_t (1 + i_{t-1}) + M_t + TR_t - T_t.\qquad(9.25)$$

Equation (9.25) holds each period and constrains the joint behavior of the monetary and fiscal authorities. B_{t+1} and M_{t+1} represent one-period bonds and money carried into period $t + 1$; i_t is the interest rate on a one-period bond issued at date t. The Fed chooses the mix of money and bonds in the hands of the public through open market operations with the goal of attaining a nominal interest rate target. I set government purchases to zero throughout.

I define the deficit for the consolidated government sector as

$$D_t = TR_t - T_t - i_{t-1}M_t.\qquad(9.26)$$

The deficit includes the revenues from money creation, sometimes referred to as the inflation tax. I will assume that the deficit, defined in this way, is an object of choice for the fiscal authority.

The budget equation can be simplified still further. Let B^T represent the total outstanding nominal debt of the government sector:

$$B_t^T = B_t + M_t.\qquad(9.27)$$

Given this notation, one can express the government budget constraint as

$$B_{t+1}^T = B_t^T (1 + i_{t-1}) + D_t.\qquad(9.28)$$

Since I assume that government purchases are zero, it follows that

$$Z_t = C_t, \qquad (9.29)$$

where Z_t is the money value of GDP.

9.1.5 THE PRICING KERNEL AND ASSET PRICES

The first-order condition for the household can be used to derive an expression for the Arrow security price $Q_t^{t+1}(S_j)$. From the state-by-state first-order conditions, aggregated over commodities,

$$Q_t^{t+1}(S_j) C_{t+1}(S_j) = \beta C_t \tilde{p}_j, \qquad (9.30)$$

where $\tilde{p}_j$ is the probability that state S_j occurs.

The assumption that there is no riskless arbitrage implies the following two relationships:

$$\sum_{j=1}^{N} Q_t^{t+1}(S_j) = \frac{1}{1+i_t}, \qquad (9.31)$$

$$\sum_{j=1}^{N} Q_t^{t+1}(S_j) \left[\frac{p_{k,t+1}(S_j) + rr_{t+1}(S_j)}{p_{k,t}} \right] = 1. \qquad (9.32)$$

Equation (9.31) is a no-arbitrage relationship between the safe return on government debt and the prices of the N Arrow securities. Equation (9.32) is a no-arbitrage relationship between capital and Arrow securities. If either of these equations *did not* hold, an agent could buy or sell Arrow securities and make a profit with no associated risk.

If there were a single state, then these equations would imply

$$1 + i_t = \frac{p_{k,t+1} + rr_{t+1}}{p_{k,t}}, \qquad (9.33)$$

which states that the return on two riskless assets must be equal. Notice that Equations (9.31) and (9.32) *do not* imply

$$1 + i_t = E_t \left[\frac{p_{k,t+1}(S_j) + rr_{t+1}(S_j)}{p_{k,t}} \right], \qquad (9.34)$$

since the Arrow security prices may be correlated with the stock price.

9.2 The Complete Model

I am now ready to describe a four-equation model that describes how GDP, the money supply, the value of employment, and the wage are related to the choice of the interest rate by the central bank. These four equations are:

$$hZ_t = i_{t-1} M_t, \qquad (9.35)$$

$$E\left[\frac{\beta Z_t}{Z_{t+1}}\right] = \frac{1}{1 + i_t}, \qquad (9.36)$$

$$E\left\{\frac{\beta Z_t}{Z_{t+1}}\left[\frac{p_{k,t+1}(S_j) + \psi Z_{t+1}(S_j)}{p_{k,t}}\right]\right\} = 1, \qquad (9.37)$$

$$\chi Z_t = w_t L_t. \qquad (9.38)$$

Equation (9.35) is the demand-for-money equation. Equations (9.36) and (9.37) are asset pricing equations that combine (9.31), and (9.32) with the pricing kernel, Equation (9.30) and the accounting identity (9.29). Equation (9.38) is the aggregate supply equation. Solving Equation (9.37) forward leads to the further simplification

$$Z_t = \frac{(1 - \beta)}{\beta \psi} p_{k,t}. \qquad (9.39)$$

Since there is a representative household, fiscal policy has no effect in this model and the fiscal authority simply chooses the timing of lump-sum taxes.

This model looks deceptively simple, but it is capable of displaying very rich nominal-real interactions. To close the model, we need to explain how agents form beliefs about the money value of stock prices, that is, the sequence $\{p_{k,t}\}$. In Chapter 10, I will explore the idea that households form self-fulfilling beliefs about the real value of assets; this assumption implies that the model is closed by an equation of the form

$$p_{k,t} = w_t x_t, \qquad (9.40)$$

where $\{x_t\}$ is a sequence of beliefs. I will show that a model with this structure behaves a lot like the new-Keynesian model used by central banks throughout the world to guide monetary policy. It differs from that model since I will allow self-fulfilling beliefs to determine unemployment and GDP in the long run.

9.3 Concluding Comments

In the real models of Part II, movements in the real stock price caused movements in the real value of consumption because the money wage was chosen to equal 1. I assumed that the *real* stock price can be any bounded sequence. In the monetary model with uncertainty, I will assume instead that the sequence $\{p_{k,t}/w_t\}$ is determined by self-fulfilling beliefs.

In Chapter 10, I will use this model to understand some of the monetary features of data since 1951.

CHAPTER 10 | Money and Inflation Since 1951

How can high inflation and high unemployment coexist? In the familiar new-Keynesian account of monetary policy discussed, for example by Richard Clarida, Jordi Galí, and Mark Gertler (2000) the Fed pays attention to deviations of unemployment from its natural rate. In the old-Keynesian model, that I describe here, there is no natural rate of unemployment and a drifting unemployment rate has big welfare consequences.

When I began work on this chapter, in early drafts of the book, I had intended to develop the dynamic implications of the theory and to study dynamic equilibria similar to those analysized by new-Keynesian economists. But as the work developed, I realized that the dynamic behavior of the old-Keynesian model is much richer than that of its new-Keynesian cousin. There is room for a new theory of expectations that is consistent with rational choice but also displays the intertial behavior that we see in real-world data. I have chosen to report the steady-state implications of the model here and to save a more complete analysis of the dynamics for a future book.

The chapter begins, in Section 10.1, with a brief review of the model. Section 10.2 describes how changes in the money wage affect unemployment. In Section 10.3, I review some features of the data and I show how they are explained by the model. In Section 10.4, I lay out the linearized old-Keynesian model, and in Section 10.5, I present a short conclusion.

10.1 A Complete Monetary Model

The monetary model, introduced in chapter 9, is described by the following four equations:

$$Q_t^{t+1} = \frac{\beta Z_t}{Z_{t+1}}, \qquad (10.1)$$

$$\beta E_t \left[\frac{Z_t}{Z_{t+1}} \right] = \frac{1}{1 + i_t}, \qquad (10.2)$$

$$E_t \left[\frac{\beta Z_t}{Z_{t+1}} \left(\frac{p_{k,t+1}(S_j) + \psi Z_{t+1}(S_j)}{p_{k,t}} \right) \right] = 1, \qquad (10.3)$$

$$\chi Z_t = w_t L_t. \qquad (10.4)$$

To study its behavior, notice that Equation (10.3) can be solved iteratively to give an expression for the value of nominal GDP as a function of the value of the stock market:

$$Z_t = p_{k,t} \frac{(1 - \beta)}{\beta \psi}. \qquad (10.5)$$

Using this expression, we may divide Equation (10.4) by $p_{k,t}$ to yield an equation linking employment to the value of the stock market measured in wage units:

$$L_t = \frac{(1 - \beta) \chi}{\beta \psi} \frac{p_{k,t}}{w_t}. \qquad (10.6)$$

One can also write GDP in wage units in this way:

$$\frac{Z_t}{w_t} = \frac{(1 - \beta)}{\psi \beta} \frac{p_{k,t}}{w_t}. \qquad (10.7)$$

Finally, one can combine the solution for GDP from Equation (10.5) with the no-arbitrage condition, Equation (10.2), to yield an expression linking the growth rate of the asset price with the interest rate:

$$\frac{1}{1 + i_t} = \beta E_t \left[\frac{p_{k,t}}{p_{k,t+1}} \right]. \qquad (10.8)$$

Since the central bank controls the money supply, it has the power to set i_t through open market operations. For any given choice of the interest rate, the implied value of the end-of-period money stock is given by the money demand equation

$$h Z_t = i_{t-1} M_t. \qquad (10.9)$$

How does the model work? I have already demonstrated that, unlike the neoclassical model, economic fundamentals are insufficient to determine either employment or GDP measured in wage units. This is expressed here by the fact that although equations (10.6) and (10.7) determine both of these variables as functions of the real stock price $p_{k,t}/w_t$, there is nothing in the economic structure of the model to pin this variable down. In addition to this real indeterminacy, the model displays the same nominal indeterminacy that one finds in any monetary model. I discuss these issues further in Section 10.4. First, I will discuss the dependence of aggregate supply on the money wage and the connection of the model with data.

10.2 Aggregate Supply and the Money Wage

How can unemployment and inflation coexist? This section gives an answer to that question. The aggregate supply function, Equation (10.4), determines Z_t as a function of w_t and L_t. When $w_t = 1$, all nominal magnitudes are in wage units. For example, the statement that good i costs $p_{i,t}$ dollars means that one unit of labor can purchase $p_{i,t}$ units of it. Scaling up the wage unit by choosing w_t to be some value other than 1 means that all money prices in the model must also be scaled up if the real value of wealth is to remain unchanged.

In Chapter 6, I described a model that determines employment, money prices, and the quantities of each produced commodity as a function of the state of long-term expectations. I modeled expectations as a bounded sequence of self-fulfilling beliefs $\{p_{k,t}\}$, where $p_{k,t}$ represents the money value of the stock market at date t. If w_t is different from 1, then these beliefs must also be scaled up or down by the money wage. If the money wage changes but beliefs about the money value of stocks do not, this change in the nominal unit will alter the real variables of the model.

Figure 10.1 illustrates how changes in the value of the nominal unit can have an adverse effect on output and employment. The figure compares two steady states. In each of them, the money value of the state of long-term expectations gives rise to a dollar price for stocks denoted p_k. When household wealth is p_k, households demand $p_k (1 - \beta) / \beta \psi$ dollars worth of goods and services. Since there is no government and no investment, aggregate consumption expenditure is equal to the money value of GDP.

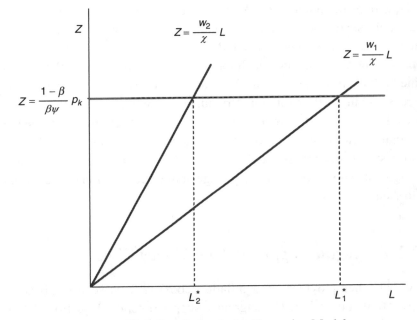

FIGURE 10.1 Stagflation in the Keynesian Model

Consider the two steady states labeled $\{w_1, L_1^*\}$ and $\{w_2, L_2^*\}$ on Figure 10.1. In the first steady state, a unit of labor costs w_1 dollars. In the second steady state, it costs w_2 dollars where, by assumption, w_2 is greater than w_1. Since the wage is higher in steady state 2, the same value of aggregate demand will purchase fewer units of labor and there will be lower employment in equilibrium. This analysis is suggestive of the phenomenon of stagflation, in which high unemployment and high inflation go together. I use the word "suggestive" because Figure 10.1 compares two steady states, whereas stagflation is a dynamic phenomenon. To complete the analysis, I will use the model developed in Section 10.1 to study how a dynamic model of inflation and unemployment can be used to explain the data.

10.3 Theory and Data

Here, I will repeat the three main equations and discuss how to supplement them with a theory of beliefs. I then compare the ways that broad trends in the data are explained by the model.

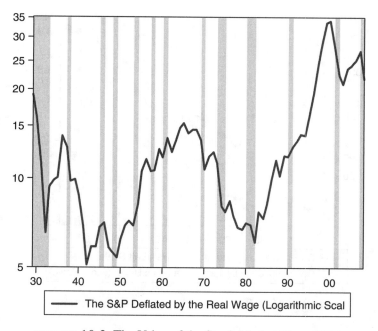

FIGURE 10.2 The Value of the Stock Market Since 1929

The three private sector equations are these:

$$L_t = \frac{(1 - \beta) \chi}{\beta \psi} \frac{p_{k,t}}{w_t}, \tag{10.10}$$

$$\frac{Z_t}{w_t} = \frac{(1 - \beta)}{\psi \beta} \frac{p_{k,t}}{w_t}, \tag{10.11}$$

$$\frac{1}{1 + i_t} = \beta E_t \left[\frac{p_{k,t}}{p_{k,t+1}} \right]. \tag{10.12}$$

I have argued that $p_{k,t}/w_t$ is a driving force of aggregate demand. How does this variable behave? The value of the S&P, deflated by the money wage, is depicted in Figure 10.2.

The data in this figure cover the period from 1929 through 2008. The hypothesis that the S&P is nonstationary cannot be rejected at the 1% level, and to capture this property, I will assume that beliefs follow a martingale; that is, I will assume that

$$E_t \left[\frac{p_{k,t+1}}{w_{t+1}} \right] = \frac{p_{k,t}}{w_t}. \tag{10.13}$$

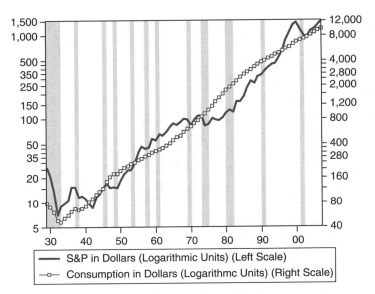

FIGURE 10.3 The Stock Market and Consumption

A second important equation in the model is (10.5), which I repeat
here:

$$Z_t = p_{k,t} \frac{(1 - \beta)}{\beta \psi}. \qquad (10.14)$$

This is the same equation that I derived in Chapter 6, in which I discussed
the Great Depression. In the model, Z_t and C_t are equal since I abstract
from investment and government purchases. In theory, it is C_t that is
determined by $p_{k,t}$, and for that reason, I have graphed the behavior
of C_t and $p_{k,t}$ in Figure 10.3. The log of the S&P is measured on the
left axis and the log of the dollar value of consumption on the right. If
Equation (10.14) holds, and if $p_{k,t}$ is a nonstationary variable driven by
beliefs, then the nominal value of consumption should be a nonstationary
variable that is cointegrated with $p_{k,t}$. Notice from the graph that these
two time series appear to grow together with a common stochastic trend,
a hypothesis that is not rejected by formal tests.[25]

The model, of course, implies more than just cointegration between
consumption and the stock market—it implies that the variables are
equal up to a scale factor. This strong implication is rejected as is clear
from Figure 10.3. It would be surprising if it were not rejected since I
have abstracted from many elements that are likely to be important in
practice. These abstractions include the representative agent assumption,
the logarithmic preference assumption, the assumption that preferences

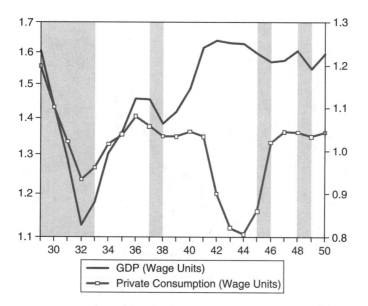

FIGURE 10.4 GDP and Consumption Before the Accord

are time separable, and the assumption that government purchases and investment are equal to zero. Any one of these factors might be responsible for providing richer dynamics to the model that would account for temporary deviations of consumption from the stock price. It would be disturbing, however, if the cointegration property were to fail, since this should be independent of assumptions that generate richer short-run dynamics.

The absence of investment or government from the model implies that GDP equals consumption. This implication is clearly false, and a model that assumed all important movements in aggregate demand were generated by movements in private consumption to understand the data during the wartime recovery would be badly off-base. The data for this period are graphed in Figure 10.4.

On this figure, GDP is graphed on the left axis and private consumption on the right. Both series are measured in wage units. Notice from the figure that GDP and consumption move in opposite directions in the 1940s. This should not be surprising since I argued in Chapter 7 that aggregate demand during WWII was driven by government purchases, a variable that is missing from the monetary model.

Figure 10.5 suggests that the approximation that demand is driven by consumption fares much better in the period from 1951 to the present. The figure plots the same two variables that were graphed on

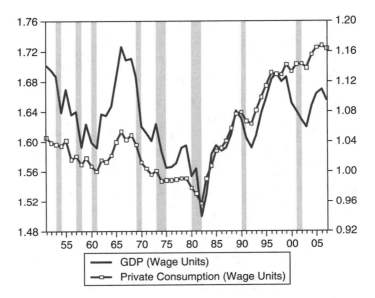

FIGURE 10.5 GDP and Consumption After the Accord

Figure 10.4 and illustrates that the important medium-term movements in postwar GDP are reflected in the consumption series. Since consumption makes up approximately 70% of GDP, one might hope that a model in which aggregate demand is purely consumption driven will

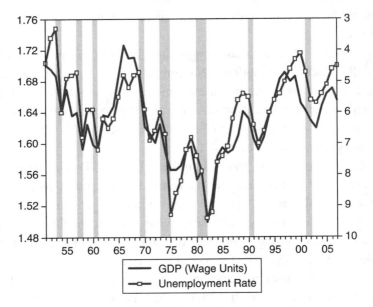

FIGURE 10.6 GDP and Unemployment

capture the most important aspects of the data; this is borne out in the figure.

A final feature that is central to the model is the equivalence of GDP measured in wage units and employment. In the model, equations (10.10) and (10.11) imply that employment is a multiple of GDP. Recall from Figure 8.4, which is replicated as Figure 10.6, that unemployment and GDP are closely correlated. This figure plots unemployment on the right scale measured from top to bottom and the real value of GDP per member of the labor force on the left axis. The assumption that these variables are equal does a very good job of explaining these data—the correlation coefficient between GDP per member of the labor force measured in wage units and the unemployment rate is -0.88.

10.4 Modeling Monetary Policy

Central bankers and academics have been guided in their discussion of monetary policy for the past decade by the new-Keynesian model of a monetary economy. This is a three equation system of linear equations in the interest rate, inflation, and GDP. My purpose in this section is to provide a similar model of an old-Keynesian economy and to draw attention to the differences between these two models. It is my hope that this old-Keynesian monetary model may prove as useful as its new-Keynesian prodecessor in providing a simple tool to help guide policy, and I plan to study its implications further in future work.

10.4.1 THE PRIVATE SECTOR EQUATIONS RESTATED

Recall that the three private sector equations are given by

$$L_t = \frac{(1 - \beta) \chi}{\beta \psi} \frac{p_{k,t}}{w_t}, \qquad (10.15)$$

$$\frac{Z_t}{w_t} = \frac{(1 - \beta)}{\psi \beta} \frac{p_{k,t}}{w_t}, \qquad (10.16)$$

$$\frac{1}{1 + i_t} = \beta E_t \left[\frac{p_{k,t}}{p_{k,t+1}} \right]. \qquad (10.17)$$

In addition, I have argued that the data are consistent with the assumption that the stock price is a martingale:

$$\frac{p_{k,t}}{w_t} = E_t \left[\frac{p_{k,t+1}}{w_{t+1}} \right].$$

(10.18)

10.4.2 THE POLICY RULE

To model monetary policy, I assume that the interest rate is set in response to changes in inflation and real economic activity:

$$(1 + i_t) = C_1 \left[\frac{w_t}{w_{t-1}} \right]^{\eta} \left[\frac{p_{k,t}}{w_t} \right]^{\lambda}.$$

(10.19)

I refer to this expression interchangeably as a central bank reaction function or a Taylor rule, after the work of John Taylor (1993). Usually, a Taylor rule is represented in terms of the response of the interest rate to deviations of inflation and the output gap from some set of predefined targets. Since these targets are not separately identified without making additional assumptions, I have collapsed them into the constant C_1.

In typical representations of the Taylor rule, the Fed responds to price inflation and the output gap. In Equation (10.19), in contrast, it reacts to wage inflation and the real stock price. These are appropriate variables to use in the context of the model and they allow me draw conclusions in a relatively simple framework. I use wage inflation rather than a price index because this is the natural model-based concept of a nominal anchor. I use the real stock price instead of output since, in the model, these variables are equal up to a constant. The Taylor rule also typically contains a term in the lagged interest rate to represent slow adjustment of the policy toward the Fed's target rate. Adding a term of this kind would enrich the dynamics of the model but would not affect the basic message of the chapter. Therefore I have excluded it.

The parameter η in Equation (10.19) represents how strongly the Fed reacts to inflation. The parameter λ measures how strongly the Fed reacts to changes in the level of economic activity. In the following section, I lay out a linearized version of this system.

10.4.3 A LINEAR APPROXIMATION

The model can be described by the following log linear representation of equations (10.15) through (10.19). A tilde over a variable denotes the natural logarithm, and b_1, b_2, b_3, and b_4 are linearization constants.

Consider first equations (10.20) through (10.22), which are approximations to (10.17) through (10.19):

$$i_t = b_1 + E_t \left[\Delta \tilde{p}_{k,t+1} \right], \tag{10.20}$$

$$\tilde{p}_{k,t} - \tilde{w}_t = E_t \left[\tilde{p}_{k,t+1} - \tilde{w}_{t+1} \right], \tag{10.21}$$

$$i_t = b_2 + \eta \left(\Delta \tilde{w}_t \right) + \lambda \left(\tilde{p}_{k,t} - \tilde{w}_t \right). \tag{10.22}$$

Δ is the first difference operator. These equations represent an independent subsystem that determines the time paths of i_t, $\tilde{p}_{k,t}$, and $\tilde{w}_t$. Given values for the stock price and the money wage, the variables $\tilde{L}_t$ and $\tilde{Z}_t$ are determined by equations (10.23) and (10.24):

$$\tilde{L}_t = \tilde{p}_{k,t} - \tilde{w}_t + b_3, \tag{10.23}$$

$$\tilde{Z}_t - \tilde{w}_t = b_4 + \tilde{p}_{k,t} - \tilde{w}_t. \tag{10.24}$$

Solving equations (10.20) through (10.22) for steady-state wage inflation, steady-state stock market appreciation, the steady-state T-bill rate, and the steady-state real value of the stock market leads to only three equations in four unknowns:

$$i = b_1 + \Delta \tilde{p}_{k,t}, \tag{10.25}$$

$$\Delta \tilde{p}_{k,t} = \Delta \tilde{w}_t, \tag{10.26}$$

$$i = b_2 + \eta \Delta w_t + \lambda \left(\tilde{p}_{k,t} - \tilde{w}_t \right). \tag{10.27}$$

This apparent indeterminacy of the model is a consequence of the underlying real structure of the economy in which the level of real economic activity is determined by the state of long-term expectations. Beliefs are represented by a self-fulfilling expectation that the stock market will be worth some amount, x; adding this belief equation closes the system:

$$\tilde{p}_{k,t} - \tilde{w}_t = x. \tag{10.28}$$

10.5 How Beliefs Influence the Unemployment Rate

This section studies the interaction of real and monetary variables in the steady state. My analysis differs from the standard new-Keynesian monetary model in a respect: In the critical old-Keynesian model there are multiple steady-state equilibria and beliefs influence the steady-state unemployment rate.

10.5.1 THE STEADY STATE

The variable x represents the value of the stock market in wage units. Given x, equations (10.25) through (10.27) can be solved for the steady-state inflation rate, which is given by the following expression:

$$\Delta \tilde{w} = \frac{b_2 - b_1}{1 - \eta} + \frac{\lambda}{1 - \eta} x. \qquad (10.29)$$

Equation (10.25) then determines the interest rate and (10.26) determines the rate of change of the stock price.

The steady-state equations are instructive, and contain an important message. The correlations in the data between inflation and real economic activity should not be independent of the way that the central bank conducts monetary policy. For example, suppose that the central bank chooses a monetary policy for which $0 < \eta < 1$. When x increases, unemployment will fall since x represents the real value of the stock market and increases in stock market wealth will increase aggregate demand and lower unemployment. Given this relationship between x and unemployment, Equation (10.29) implies that we should observe a Phillips curve (a relationship between unemployment and wage inflation) with a negative slope. If investors become more optimistic (an increase in x), Equation (10.23) implies that employment will increase (unemployment will fall) and Equation (10.29) implies that this fall in unemployment will be associated with an increase in inflation. If on the other hand, $\eta > 1$, the steady state Phillips curve will have the opposite slope.

10.5.2 ACTIVE AND PASSIVE MONETARY POLICY

In addition to the real steady-state indeterminacy discussed previously, this model also displays a dynamic indeterminacy for certain kinds of Fed policies. I will discuss this idea further in this section and I will present an argument, due to Clarida and colleagues (2000), who claimed in the context of the new-Keynesian model of monetary policy that the Fed brought inflation under control by enacting a more aggressive monetary policy after 1980 than before. Following Eric Leeper (1991), a policy in which $0 < \eta < 1$ is called passive and one in which $\eta > 1$ is called active. A considerable amount of evidence in recent years has pointed

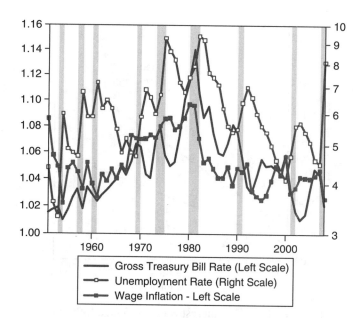

FIGURE 10.7 Unemployment, Inflation, and the Interest Rate

to the fact that U.S. monetary policy was passive before 1980 and active thereafter. This evidence is illustrated by figures 10.7 and 10.8.

Figure 10.7 displays the behavior of wage inflation, the interest rate, and inflation from 1951 through 2007. Notice that all three variables trend upward from 1951 through 1979 and that, beginning in 1980, they trend down. According to a leading explanation of these data, due to Clarida and colleagues (2000) the turnaround in these trends occurred because the Fed switched policies in 1980 when Paul Volcker became chairman.

Figure 10.8 is a scatter plot of the gross interest rate on Treasury bills against the gross rate of wage inflation for the period from 1951 through 2007. On this figure, the data for the period from 1951 through 1979 are plotted as open circles, and the data for 1980 throught 2007 appear as shaded squares. For each subperiod, I have drawn the least squares line through the points. The best line through the first subperiod has a slope of 0.78, while the best line through the second subperiod has a slope of 1.35. These numbers have been interpreted in the literature on new-Keynesian economics as estimates of η, the slope of the policy rule. Although least squares is likely to provide a biased estimate of η, alternative estimates of η using instrumental variables by Clarida and colleagues (2000) and using Bayesian techniques in a complete model by

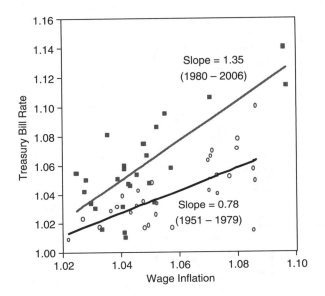

FIGURE 10.8 The Interest Rate and Wage Inflation

Lubik and Schorfheide (2004) have established similar results. Monetaty policy was passive before 1980 and active thereafter.

In the new-Keynesian model studied by Clarida and colleagues (2000), a passive monetary policy leads to dynamic indeterminacy. In that model, there is a unique natural unemployment rate. The actual unemployment rate may deviate temporarily from its natural rate because prices are sticky. Clarida and colleagues show that an active monetary policy is sufficient under some additional assumptions to ensure that the path back to full employment, following a shock, is unique. If monetary policy is passive, in contrast, there are many possible dynamic paths leading back to full employment.

The model described in this book also displays dynamic indeterminacy for some kinds of monetary policy. This dynamic indeteminacy is in addition to the steady-state indeterminacy that follows from the labor market search externality described in Part I.

10.6 Concluding Comments

This chapter integrated monetary theory into a representative agent model with Keynesian unemployment. The resulting model has a contin-uum of real equilibria, indexed by beliefs, but each of them is consistent with any steady-state equilibrium rate of inflation. I refer to this model as old-Keynesian, to distinguish it from the new-Keynesian model, widely used by central bankers and academics to study monetary policy. What does the job of the Fed look like in the old-Keynesian world?

From the viewpoint of a monetary authority, armed with the tool of interest rate control, the old-Keynesian model described in this chapter is very similar to the new-Keynesian model that has been popular recently among academics and central bankers. The difference is that in the new-Keynesian model permanent shocks to the unemployment rate are viewed as changes in the natural rate of unemployment that do not carry welfare implications.

In the new-Keynesian world, there is nothing demand management policy can or should do about increases in the natural rate. In the old-Keynesian world, there is nothing natural about any given unemployment rate and if unemployment moves above or below the social optimum, demand management policy can and should try to move it back. The fact that movements in the unemployment rate are a bad thing that should be prevented does not mean, however, that monetary policy, operating through interest rate control, is the best tool for the job. Interest rate policy has been used to alleviate recessions. But it also affects inflation. The following chapter suggests an alternative tool of monetary policy that may be used to separate these two goals.

CHAPTER 11 | How to Fix the Economy

IN THIS BOOK, I have contrasted two competing visions of the macroeconomy. In the first, an unregulated capitalist economy converges quickly to a social optimum. In the second, an unregulated capitalist economy can lead to very bad outcomes that persist for decades. This book has argued that the second view is a more accurate description of the world. Although capitalism has much to recommend it, we do not live in an unregulated economy and we have not done so since the turn of the nineteenth century. Modern political institutions are designed to improve human welfare by moderating the swings of business cycles. Modern economic theory cannot explain why this is worth doing since both classical and new-Keynesian explanations of the business cycle imply that the welfare costs of recessions are trivial.

This book has brought Keynesian theory into the twenty-first century by integrating it with general equilibrium theory in a new way and by providing microfoundations to the Keynesian theories of aggregate supply and aggregate demand. My explanation is neither classical nor new-Keynesian. It is old-Keynesian. By grounding Keynes's theory of aggregate supply in the theory of labor market search, I am able to explain why the money wage does not fall to restore employment to its socially optimal level. By grounding aggregate demand in the theory of dynamic choice under uncertainty, I am able to explain the economic history of the twentieth century in a new way.

Keynesian economics provides two remedies to unemployment: monetary and fiscal policy. Since the money interest rate was already close to zero in the 1930s, it was not possible to lower the interest rate further to increase aggregate demand. Hence, Keynes favored fiscal policy, and his theory of the multiplier explained how this would work. The theory developed here explains why fiscal policy was effective. In this chapter, I will argue that although expansionary fiscal policy can restore full employment, there is a more effective way to maintain full employment that does not burden future generations with government debt.

Let me be clear about the premise that underlies the arguments I will make. In a view shared by many academics at the very best universities and research institutes in the world, business fluctuations are efficient responses of the market system to random shocks to fundamentals. In a second view that I have put forward in this book, business fluctuations are inefficient reallocations of labor between market and nonmarket activities that arise from the unpredictable movements of market psychology. If the first view is correct, there is no role for government policy and the proper response of government is to leave well alone. If the second view is correct, government should act to maintain full employment and the central bank should promote a stable value for the currency. It will be clear by now that I favor the second view. However, I have misgivings about current approaches to the problem of maintaining full employment that I explain here.

11.1 Monetary Policy Cannot Hit Two Targets

In some currency areas (for example, Europe), the central bank is charged solely with maintaining a stable value for the currency. In others (for example, the United States), the central bank is charged both with maintaining the value of the currency and with preventing recessions. These two goals may sometimes conflict.

Central banks throughout the world have, for the past fifteen years, been guided by new-Keynesian economics. This doctrine was developed from ideas of Paul Samuelson who, in the third edition of his textbook (1955), introduced the neoclassical synthesis. In Samuelson's scheme, the economy converges, in the long run, to a full employment equilibrium. It may deviate from full employment in the short run because prices are slow to adjust. The new-Keynesians adopted this idea and developed it further. In new-Keynesian economics, there may be a short-run role for monetary policy to stimulate employment, but in the long run, monetary policy cannot influence the natural rate of unemployment. It is for this reason that the European Central Bank has been given the mandate to control inflation but not to intervene to influence the level of economic activity. It is widely believed that central banks cannot influence unemployment in the long run, and some have argued that the attempt to influence it in the short run will lead to a policy that unleashes inflationary pressures and is counterproductive.

The conflicting goals of monetary policy are apparent as I write. In 2008, there was a large fall in U.S. household wealth triggered by a drop in the price of houses. This fall in wealth was transferred throughout the world through a newly developed market for mortgage-backed securities that allowed assets, backed by the U.S. housing market, to be purchased by financial institutions throughout the globe. As the prices of U.S. houses collapsed, these assets lost value and global demand for goods and services fell. At the same time, world markets experienced unprecedented increases in raw materials prices that were fueled by the growth of China and India. A scenario is being repeated that we last saw in the 1970s. A series of cost shocks that are putting upward pressure on domestic prices have coincided with a fall in asset prices that have reduced consumer demand.

The fallout from the housing crisis is global, but it has been addressed differently in Europe and the United States. In the U.S., the Fed responded by lowering the interest rate in an attempt to stimulate demand. The Bank of England and the European Central Bank took a more aggressive stance against inflation, and interest rates in Europe and the United Kingdom came down more slowly. Central bankers there were initially more concerned with the long-term consequences of allowing inflation to build. The contradictory responses to similar events illustrates the trade off between conflicting goals of monetary policy. A single instrument, the interest rate, cannot be used to hit two targets.

11.2 Fiscal Policy Is Not the Most Effective Solution

During the Great Depression, Keynes argued that the government should purchase goods and services and pay for its increased expenditure by borrowing from households. This policy was designed to increase aggregate demand. Expansionary fiscal policy was successful at increasing employment during World War II, but the huge increase in government purchases that occurred to finance the war was accompanied by a big permanent increase in the scale of government.

Fiscal policy may be effective at increasing employment, but it is not the best response to a recession for two reasons. In the textbook view of Keynesian economics (Samuelson, 1955), a fiscal expansion involves some combination of a cut in taxes, an increase in government purchases, and an increase in transfers to individuals. The most effective package is one in which a tax cut is accompanied by an increase in government purchases. A policy of this kind will increase aggregate demand by more than a transfer to individuals since, in textbook Keynesianism, households will save part of the transfer whereas government spends it all. But there are also disadvantages to an increase in government purchases, since most individuals would prefer to choose how to spend their income rather than have it spent for them. I do not deny that there is a role for government to provide public goods—defense and the legal system are good examples—but the percentage of GDP that a society devotes to government activities should not be changed in arbitrary ways to stimulate the economy during recessions.

This leaves transfers to the public, financed by borrowing, as a possible remedy. In the housing crisis of 2008, the U.S. government enacted a tax rebate that returned checks of between $600 and $1,200 to most families. This policy may have helped to delay the onset of a recession in the U.S., but it was at the cost of increasing the national debt. Since government debt is the liability of future generations, a transfer policy of this kind can only be effective by redistributing resources from one generation to another. This was the message of chapters 6 and 7, in which I showed how the wartime recovery could be explained by a model that recognizes that debt is a transfer between generations. In the extreme case in which households fully discount future tax liabilities, a tax rebate of this kind can have no effect on aggregate employment.

Let me recap the two strikes against fiscal policy as a weapon to combat recessions. First, even if one accepts the mechanics that Samuelson explained in his interpretation of Keynes, and even if the government can increase employment, the resulting equilibrium will be second best since the choices of consumers have been replaced by those of the state. Second, for a given state of long-term expectations, government intervention through increased expenditure may get only partway back to full employment. The effectiveness of the intervention depends on the ability to make transfers between different groups. As I write this book, we are about to enter a recession at a time when the public purse is stretched to pay for a war in the Middle East. Additional government, debt will place a costly burden on future generations who are already facing significant costs as the baby boom generation ages and tax revenues from the working population begin to shrink. Perhaps we can do better than this?

11.3 What We Should Do Instead

I am going to present a different idea; I will argue that government should expand the role of the Fed. Currently, the Central Bank meets eight times a year and at each meeting the open market committee decides on a target at which to set the interest rate on federal funds. To achieve any given target, the Federal Reserve Bank of New York is charged with the task of buying or selling securities on the open market to raise or lower the interest rate. Historically, open market operations have been conducted by buying or selling treasury bills. In January 2008, the Fed's assets were approximately $850 billion, which was roughly 7% of GDP, and until the summer of 2008, almost all of these assets were held as high-grade government securities. In the credit crisis of 2008, the Fed expanded credit to a number of institutions by accepting lower grade securities as collateral, and by September 2008, about a third of the Fed's portfolio was of this form. Why did it follow this policy?

From 2004 through July 2007, the Fed was more concerned about inflation than about a recession, and during this period the federal funds rate increased from 1% in May 2004 to 5.25% in July 2007. In August 2007, the Fed began a series of rate cuts, and by May 2008, the federal funds rate was down to 2%. During this period, the Fed expanded credit through open market operations by approximately $30 billion and it cut the federal funds rate by 325 basis points. By spring 2009, these policies had resulted in a doubling of the stock of high-powered money from $850 billion to $1.8 trillion.

In normal times, changes in the federal funds rate cause similar movements in a whole spectrum of rates of return. If the Fed is willing to pay less on overnight loans, then lower grade securities also pay less and the spread between assets of different grades remains approximately constant. But in depressions, the spread on different assets widens. This happened in the Great Depression and it happened again in 2008. Although the Fed aggressively lowered the federal funds rate, the interest rate on securities backed by subprime mortgages continued to fall in price and institutions that held large portfolios of these assets were unable to trade them. As the Fed increased liquidity in the markets, the price of securities backed by subprime mortgages did not respond. Instead, the spread between AAA bonds and mortgage-backed securities remained high. The Fed was faced with the possibility of the collapse of one or more major financial institutions and to prevent this from occurring, it began to accept lower grade securities as collateral for Federal Reserve loans.

The fraction of Federal Reserve assets backed by high-grade government securities has been 90% or greater since at least 1996, but by July 2008, it had fallen to 50%. The decision to begin buying lower grade securities was a bold new move by the Bernanke Fed. Economists often talk as if there was a single interest rate. In practice, there is a whole spectrum of assets, each of which pays a different rate of return. By agreeing to hold a portfolio of different securities, the Fed embarked on a path in which it can potentially control not just one rate of return, but several. This is a logical development of the role of the central bank and it is a path that leads to an expanded role for the Fed as a guarantor not just of the value of the currency but also of the unemployment rate. I will explain what I mean by this in the following section.

11.4 A New Role for the Fed

In the late 1990s, the public lost confidence in the value of stocks, but housing wealth appreciated. The 2008 recession is different because households lost confidence in stocks and houses simultaneously. The destruction of household wealth had a disastrous effect on aggregate demand. What can we do about it? We need to support the value of wealth through direct intervention in the asset markets.

One way of achieving this goal is for the Fed to vary not just the size but also the composition of its balance sheet. Under my proposal, the Fed would define a basket of securities; ideally, this would include all publicly traded stocks weighted by market capitalization. The exact composition of the basket is not important. What matters is that it is known and fixed. Just as the Fed controls the price of overnight borrowing by buying and selling government debt in the open market, the Fed would stand ready to buy and sell shares in index funds.

The Fed open market committee meets eight times a year to decide the interest rate on federal funds. In addition to setting the interest rate, the open market committee would announce a price at which it would stand willing to buy or sell shares of the index fund and a rate of growth at which this price would increase daily over the next month.

Initially, the Fed would encourage private companies such as Vanguard or Fidelity to create index funds and it would buy an initial block of shares at market prices. To pay for these shares, it would issue its own fixed interest liabilities that would be directly guaranteed by the Treasury. The open market committee would act to maintain the real value of the fund price within a set of bounds to prevent bubbles and stop market crashes. It would not have the mandate to intervene by buying and selling individual corporations—only the index fund.

How big would the purchase of shares need to be? In theory, the mere statement that the government stands ready to buy and sell at a fixed price should be enough to stabilize the markets. In practice, the balance sheet of the Fed was about $850 billion at the end of 2008 and an increase of a further $850 billion seems about right. This increase would not affect the money supply since it would be paid for by issuing debt. To support the markets in time of panics, the Fed would have the ability to buy additional shares on the open market. To dampen the market during bubbles, it would be able to sell back its own portfolio or, if that were to prove insufficient, it could design a financial instrument that pays the same return as the index fund and sell this instrument on the market.

Since the return to stocks has historically outpaced government debt by 5 percentage points, the Fed might make a sizeable profit for the government. I think this is unlikely. A more plausible scenario is that, when the extreme swings of market volatility become part of the history of capitalism, the returns to debt and equity will move closer together and the equity premium will be eliminated or considerably reduced.

Coming from a classical perspective, the proposal sounds irresponsible at best. Surely the market will go wherever it wants to go to find the correct fundamental value of underlying assets. I do not believe that this is the correct theory of stock market value, and the extreme swings in volatility that we observe in market valuation are not, in my view, reflections of changes in a unique underlying fundamental valuation. They are caused by self-fulfilling swings in confidence.

The plan I have advocated does not make sense in a classical environment with a unique natural rate of unemployment and a self-stabilizing market system. But that is not the world in which we live. I believe instead that there are many possible equilibrium unemployment rates and the one we end up with is determined by demand. By placing a floor and a ceiling on the value of swings in stock market valuation, the Fed will nudge the market back toward a valuation that maintains a more stable growth rate for private wealth. By stabilizing wealth, the Fed will maintain a predictable environment for private investors to create jobs and a stable environment for households to plan for the future. My goal is to preserve capitalism as an engine of growth without stifling entrepreneurship.

11.5 Concluding Comments

When I began writing this book in 2005, the arguments were academic. I had long felt that the new-Keynesians misrepresented the main message of *The General Theory*. It was my intention to recast this message in the language of modern equilibrium economics. At the outset, I thought that I was rescuing Keynesian economics. As the work progressed, I realized that Keynesian economics was not only misinterpreted but, in places, it was simply wrong. One example is Keynes's theory of prices that was at best poorly developed. A second was his theory of the labor market that was nonexistent in the sense that we understand what is meant by a good theory in modern economics. When I began to construct a theory that is consistent with the message of *The General Theory*, it became apparent that the Keynesian remedy of fiscal deficits can be improved upon.

In the fall of 2008, a work that began as purely academic quickly took on an urgency and I discovered a new purpose that goes well beyond my original intention. In September 2008, financial institutions throughout the world began to fail, and by some accounts the capitalized value of world stock markets fell by 50% in the space of six weeks. This crisis led economists, journalists, politicians, and commentators to search for new explanations. Some observers are returning to Keynesian economics: Others are searching for classical explanations. The news media is full of talking heads with plausible explanations for the crisis and what to do about it, but none of the existing accounts provides a plausible explanation for why capitalist economies usually function smoothly but at times can go spectacularly wrong. There are stories—but none that holds water as an account of the specific market failure that justifies when and how there is a role for government intervention. In this book, I have given an account of the functioning of the market system that explains what this market failure is and how to correct it.

NOTES

1. Galí, Gertler, and Salido (2007, p. 56) find that the average welfare costs of business fluctuations in a new-Keynesian model are approximately 0.01% of steady-state consumption, a number that is consistent with that cited by Lucas (1987, Chapter IV) in the context of the real business cycle model.

2. There appears to be a long history of misattributions of this quote. In private correspondence, Riccardo DiCecio made the following observation: My colleague Ed Nelson pointed out to me that the phrase "We are all Keynesians now" attributed to Pres. Nixon is from Milton Friedman and is incomplete. Nixon said, "I'm now a Keynesian in economics," according to journalist Howard K. Smith. Friedman, in an interview with *Time*, said, "In one sense, we are all Keynesians now; in another, no one is a Keynesian any longer." However, *Time* magazine only quoted, "We are all Keynesians now."

3. Keth Carlson and Roger Spencer (1975) have an early comprehensive discussion of the crowding-out debate.

4. I am not the first to suggest that medium-term movements might be important features of the business cycle. In a recent article in the *American Economic Review*, Diego Comin and Mark Gertler (2006) have drawn attention to postwar medium-term fluctuations that they attribute to endogenous productivity movements.

5. q is closely related to labor market tightness, which Mortensen and Pissarides (1994) define to be the ratio of vacancies to unemployment.

6. In a dynamic model, employment will appear as a state variable in a programming problem since it takes time to recruit new workers. In this book, I abstract from this aspect of labor market dynamics.

7. The main reason why unemployment is so high in the planning optimum is my assumption that labor is fired and rehired every period.

8. This is actually two figures superimposed since I am measuring both monetary and real units on the vertical axis. The function $Z = \phi(L)$ has units of dollars and the function $Y = \psi(L)$ is in units of commodities.

9. It is for precisely this reason that Keynes called his book *The General Theory*. He viewed the Walrasian equilibrium as one of many possible rest points of the system.

10. A version of this chapter appeared in the *International Journal of Economic Theory* (2008a) and is reprinted here with permission.

11. The fact that L^* is equal to $1/2$ follows from the assumption that the elasticity of the matching function is 0.5.

12. The quote is from *Through the Looking Glass: And What Alice Found There"*, by Lewis Carroll, Chapter 6. I am indebted to Riccardo DiCecio for correcting a misattribution of this quote in an earlier draft of this manuscript.

13. I will abstract here from the bequest motive for saving. Adding bequests will not change the main message of the book provided bequests are given because the giver obtains direct utility from the size of the gift.

14. I have called this full employment in line with the language of *The General Theory* although the model introduced here admits of overemployment as well as underemployment.

15. Hodrick and Prescott. (1997).

16. A second objection to the use of filtered data is one that is often raised by those who favor a traditional econometric approach to the analysis of time series data. Since the filter is two sided, it is not consistent to assume that filtered data can be modeled "as if" it were chosen by a forward-looking rational agent operating in a world with no trend in productivity. Despite this objection, a number of influential papers do use HP-filtered data in this way.

17. This is a nonstandard definition since wealth would normally be defined as the net present value of the labor endowment. Here it is the net present value of labor income.

18. In her Ph.D. thesis, Amy Brown (2010, expected) shows that for the same matching function used here, the socially efficient unemployment rate can be as low as 3% if all workers are not fired and rehired every period.

19. Carlson and Spencer (1975).

20. The interest rate, in this model, must be non-negative and, since the growth rate is zero, this condition rules out dynamic inefficiency of the kind that is known to occur in overlapping generations models under some conditions. See Karl Shell (1971).

21. There is no presumption that the economy was at the social planning optimum in 1929. I have nevertheless chosen this starting point for illustrative purposes.

22. Marianne Baxter and Robert G. King (1999) compare the band-pass filter to alternative detrending methods.

23. The government debt series has units of pure numbers and the deflated S&P series has units of inverse dollars dated at the inception year of the index. The contribution of the S&P to aggregate wealth depends on this dollar value that is unknown, and hence the *level* of the series reported in Figure 8.6 is not directly comparable to the level of the debt series, although the *movements* in the two series, *can* be directly compared.

24. This part of the model draws on a recent working paper with Carine Nourry and Alain Venditti (2009) from the Groupement de Recherche en Économie Quantitative d'Aix-Marseille (GREQAM), in which we developed a stochastic model of long-lived agents. Farmer, Nourry, and Venditti (2009).

25. One cannot reject the hypothesis that each series is nonstationary. Further, one cannot reject the hypothesis that they are cointegrated at the 5% level using a Johansen cointegration test and imposing the assumption of no deterministic trend.

BIBLIOGRAPHY

Azariadis, C. (1981): "Self-Fulfilling Prophecies," *Journal of Economic Theory,* 25, 380–396.

Barro, R. J. (1974): "Are Government Bonds Net Wealth?" *Journal of Political Economy*, 82(6), 1095–1117.

Barro, R. J., and H. Grossman (1971): "A General Disequilibrium Model of Income and Employment," *American Economic Review*, 61, 82–93.

Baxter, M., and R. G. King (1999): "Measuring Business Cycles: Approximate Band-Pass Filters for Economic Time Series," *Review of Economics and Statistics*, 81(November), 575–593.

Benassy, J. P. (1975): "Neo-Keynesian Disequilibrium Theory in a Monetary Economy," *Review of Economic Studies*, 42, 503–523.

Benhabib, J., and R. E. A. Farmer (1994): "Indeterminacy and Increasing Returns," *Journal of Economic Theory,* 63(1), 19–41.

Beyer, A., and R. E. A. Farmer (2007), "Natural Rate Doubts," *Journal of Economic Dynamics and Control,* 31, 797–825.

Blanchard, O. J. (1985): "Debts, Deficits, and Finite Horizons," *Journal of Political Economy*, 93(April), 223–247.

Brown, A. (2010, expected): "Three Essays in Macroeconomics" (Working title), Ph.D. thesis, UCLA.

Carlson, K. M., and R. W. Spencer (1975): "Crowding Out and Its Critics," *Federal Reserve Bank of St. Louis*, December, 2–16.

Cass, D., and Karl Shell (1983): "Do Sunspots Matter," *Journal of Political Economy*, 91, 193–227.

Clarida, R., J. Galí, and M. Gertler (2000): "Monetary Policy Rules and Macroeconomic Stability: Evidence and Some Theory," *Quarterly Journal of Economics*, 115(1), 147–180.

Clower, R. W. (1965): "The Keynesian Counterrevolution: A Theoretical Appraisal," in *The Theory of Interest Rates*, ed. by F. Hahn and F. Brechling. McMillan, London.

Cole, H. L., and L. E. Ohanian (2004): "New Deal Policies and the Persistence of the Great Depression: A General Equilibrium Analysis," *Journal of Political Economy*, 112(4), 779–816.

Comin, D., and M. Gertler (2006): "Medium Term Business Cycles," *American Economic Review*, 96(3), 523–551.

Diamond, P. A. (1982): "Aggregate Demand Management in Search Equilibrium," *Journal of Political Economy*, 90, 881–894.

———(1984): "Money in Search Equilibrium," *Econometrica*, 52, 1–20.

Dreze, J. H. (1975): "Existence of an Exchange Economy with Price Rigidities," *International Economic Review*, 16, 310–320.

Evans, G. W., and S. Honkapohja (2001): *Learning and Expectations in Macroeconomics*. Princeton University Press, Princeton.

Farmer, R. E. A. (1984): "A New Theory of Aggregate Supply," *American Economic Review*, 74(5), 920–929.

———(1991): "Sticky Prices," *Economic Journal*, 101(409), 1369–1379.

———(1999): *The Macroeconomics of Self-Fulfilling Prophecies*. MIT Press, Cambridge, MA, second edn.

———(2002): "Fiscal Policy. Equity Premia and Heterogeneous Agents," UCLA mimeo, May.

———(2008a): "Aggregate Demand and Supply," *International Journal of Economic Theory*, 4(1), 77–94.

———(2008b): "Old Keynesian Economics," in *Macroeconomics in the Small and the Large*, Roger E. A. Farmer ed., Edward Elgar, London.

Farmer, R. E. A., and J. T. Guo (1994): "Real Business Cycles and the Animal Spirits Hypothesis," *Journal of Economic Theory*, 63(1), 42–72.

———(1995): "The Econometrics of Indeterminacy," *The Carnegie Rochester Conference Series on Public Policy*, 43, 225–272.

Farmer, R.E.A., C. Nourry and A. Venditti (2009): "Debt Deficits and Finite Horizons, the Stochastic Case", NBER WP15025.

Friedman, M. (1948): "A Monetary and Fiscal Framework for Economic Stability," *American Economic Review*, 38(June), 245–264.

———(1956): "The Quantity Theory of Money—A Restatement," in *Studies in the Quantity Theory of Money*, ed. by M. Friedman. University of Chicago Press, Chicago.

———(1957): *A Theory of the Consumption Function*. Princeton University Press, Princeton.

———(1968): "The Role of Monetary Policy," *American Economic Review*, 58(March), 1–17.

Friedman, M., and A. J. Schwartz (1963): *A Monetary History of the United States, 1867–1960*. Princeton University Press, Princeton.

Galí, J., M. Gertler, and D. L. Salido (2007): "Markups, Gaps and the Welfare Costs of Business Cycle Fluctuations," *Review of Economics and Statistics*, 89(1), 44–59.

Haberler, G. (1937): *Prosperity and Depression*. George Allen and Unwin Ltd, London.

Hall, R. E. (2005): "Employment Fluctuations with Equilibrium Wage Stickiness," *American Economic Review*, 95(1), 50–65.

Harrison, S., and M. Weder. (2006): "Did Sunspot Forces Cause the Great Depression?" *Journal of Monetary Economics*, 53, 1527–1539.

Hodrick, R. J., and E. C. Prescott. (1997): "Post-War U.S. Business cycles: A Descriptive Empirical Investigation," *Journal of Money Credit and Banking*, 29, 1–16.

Howitt, P. (1986): "The Keynesian Recovery," *Canadian Journal of Economics*, 19(4), 626–641.

Howitt, P., and R. P. McAfee (1987): "Costly Search and Recruiting," *International Economic Review*, 28(1), 89–107.

Kehoe, T. J., and E. C. Prescott (2007): *Great Depressions of the Twentieth Century*. Federal Reserve Bank of Minneapolis, Minneapolis, MN.

Keynes, J. M. (1936): *The General Theory of Employment, Interest and Money*. MacMillan and Co, London.

———(1937): "The General Theory of Employment," *Quarterly Journal of Economics*, 51(2) 209–223.

Kuhn, T.S. (1962): *The Structure of Scientific Revolutions*. University of Chicago Press, Chicago II.

Kydland, F. E., and E. C. Prescott (1982): "Time to Build and Aggregate Fluctuations," *Econometrica*, 50, 1345–1370.

———(1996): "The Computational Experiment: An Econometric Tool," *Journal of Economic Perspectives*, 10(Winter), 69–85.

Lavington, F. (1922): *The Trade Cycle*. P.S. King and Son, London.

Leeper, E. M. (1991): "Equilibria Under 'Active' and 'Passive' Monetary and Fiscal Policies," *Journal of Monetary Economics*, 27(1), 129–147.

Leijonhufvud, A. (1966): *On Keynesian Economics and the Economics of Keynes*. Oxford University Press, New York.

Lubik, T. A., and F. Schorfheide (2004): "Testing for Indeterminacy: An Application to U.S. Monetary Policy," *American Economic Review*, 94(1), 190–219.

Lucas Jr., R. E. (1967): "Optimal Investment Policy and the Flexible Accelerator," *International Economic Review*, 8, 78–85.

———(1972): "Expectations and the Neutrality of Money," *Journal of Economic Theory*, 4, 103–124.

———(1976): "Econometric Pdicy Evaluation: A Critique", Carnegie Rochester Conference Series on Public Policy, North Holland, 104–130.

———(1987): *Models of Business Cycles*. Basil Blackwell, Oxford, UK.

Lucas Jr., R. E., and L. A. Rapping (1969): "Real Wages Employment and Inflation," *Journal of Political Economy*, 77, 721–754.

Lucas Jr., R. E., and T. J. Sargent (1981): *Rational Expectations and Econometric Practice*. University of Minnesota Press, Minneapolis, MN.

Malinvaud, E. (1977): *The Theory of Unemployment Reconsidered*. Basil Blackwell, Oxford, UK.

Moen, E. (1997): "Competitive Search Equilibrium," *Journal of Political Economy*, 105(2), 385–411.

Mortensen, D. T., and C. Pissarides (1994): "Job Creation and Job Destruction in the Theory of Unemployment," *Review of Economic Studies*, 61, 397–415.

Patinkin, D. (1956): *Money Interest and Prices (3rd ed. 1989)*. MIT Press, Cambridge, MA, second abridged ed.

Phelps, E.S. (1968): "Money Wage Dynamics and Labor Market Equilibrium," *Journal of Polittical Economy*, 76, 678–711.

――― (1970): "The New Microeconomics in Inflation and Employment Theory," in *Microeconomic Foundations of Employment and Inflation Theory*, ed. by E. S. Phelps. Norton, New York.

Pigou, A. C. (1929): *Industrial Fluctuations*. McMillan, London.

Pissarides, C. (2000): *Equilibrium Unemployment Theory*. MIT Press, Cambridge, MA, 2nd ed.

Rogerson, R., R. Shimer, and R. Wright (2005): "Search-Theoretic Models of the Labor Market: A Survey," *Journal of Economic Literature*, 43, 959–988.

Samuelson, P. A. (1955): *Economics: An Introductory Analysis*. . McGraw Hill, third ed., New York.

――― (1958): "An Exact Consumption-Loan Model of Interest With or Without the Social Contrivance of Money," *Journal of Political Economy*, 66(December), 467–482.

Santayana, G. (1905): *The Life of Reason*. C Scribner's Sons, New York.

Shell, K. (1971): "Notes on the Economics of Infinity," *Journal of Political Economy*, 79, 1002–1011.

Shimer, R. (1996): "Contracts in a Frictional Labor Market," Unpublished manuscript.

――― (2005): "The Cyclical Behavior of Equilibrium Unemployment and Vacancies," *American Economic Review*, 95(1), 25–49.

Taylor, J. B. (1993): "Discretion versus Policy Rules in Practice," *Carnegie Rochester Conference Series on Public Policy*, 39, 195–214.

Treadway, A. B. (1971): "The Rational Multivariate Flexible Accelerator," *Econometrica*, 39(5), 845–855.

Weil, P. (1989): "Overlapping Generations of Infinitely Lived Agents," *Journal of Public Economics*, 38, 183–198.

Yaari, M. E. (1965): "Uncertain Lifetime, Life Insurance, and the Theory of the Consumer," *Review of Economic Studies*, 32, 137–150.

INDEX

Taylor rule, 160
Taylor, J. B., 160
total factor productivity, 6
total wealth, 85
Treadway, A. B., 82
treasury bill (T-bill), 4, 80, 127–129, 161, 163, 171

underemployment, 45, 60, 62, 178 (*see also* overemployment)
unemployment, 3–5, 11–13, 28, 49, 56, 71–79, 81–82, 91, 95–98, 102, 105, 105, 122, 127–128, 131–135, 139, 143, 149, 151, 153–154, 159, 162, 165, 167, 169, 172, 177–178
  equilibrium level of, 3
  inefficiently high level of, 15, 95
  natural rate of, 4, 73, 134–135, 138, 151, 164–165, 169, 174
  volatility of, 9
unit of account, 65
unit of monetary value, 34
unit of ordinary labor, 33–34

vacancies, 15–16, 19, 21, 30, 177
  volatility of, 9
value of equity, 89

Venditti, A., 179
Vietnam War, 129, 137
Volcker, P., 80, 163

wage, 7–9, 15–17, 20–21, 24–26, 29–31, 33, 53, 63, 73–75, 89, 111, 127–129, 143, 149, 154, 160–163
wage units, 28, 46, 69, 72–73, 75–76, 80, 94, 98, 103, 111, 114, 120, 129, 131–133, 136–137, 152–153, 157, 159, 162
Walrasian
  general equilibrium theory, 48–49, 63, 178
  market, 30
wartime recovery, 13, 67, 98, 109–110, 116, 119–120, 122, 157, 170
wealth effect, 96, 120, 122
Weder, M., 90
Weil, P., 115
welfare theorems, 15
Wharton model, 70
World War II (WWII), 95–96, 98, 122, 127, 157, 170
Wright, R., 21

Yaari, M. E., 109, 118, 120